FORECLOSURE AND SHORT SALE

How To Make Money With A Situation That You Thought Was Going To Ruin Your Life

NERIO MACHADO

FORECLOSURE AND SHORT-SALE

1ST EDITION

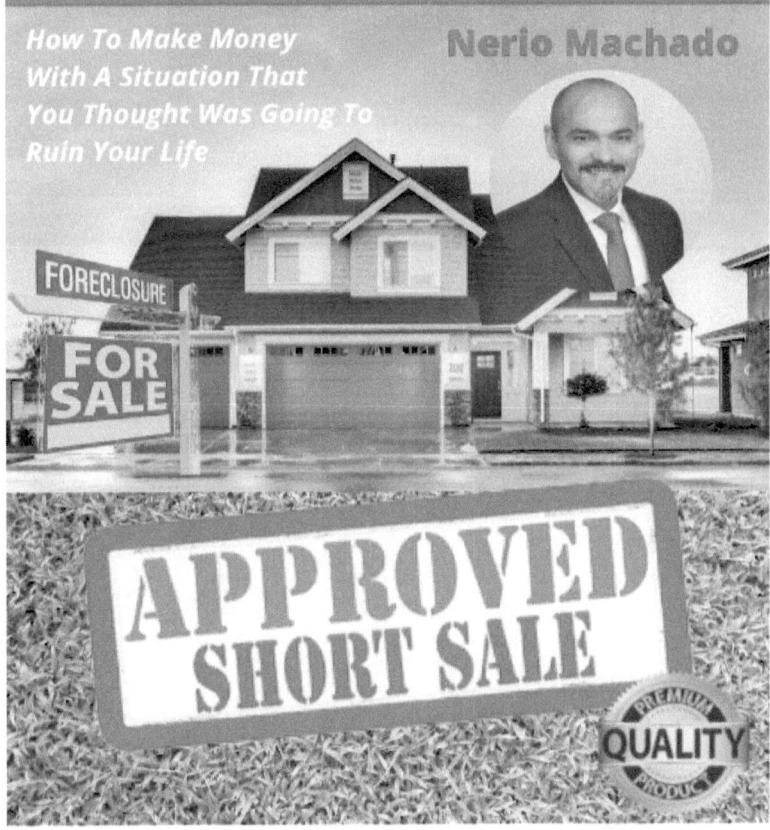

Nerio Machado + Real Estate Agent

✉ neriomachadorealtor@gmail.com

📷 @machadoteam
　Nerio Machado

f @neriomachadorealtor
　Nerio Machado

▶ Nerio Machado

🌐 www.machadoteam.com

CONTENT

Introduction - 7

CHAPTER I: Foreclosure

1. Foreclosure - 15
2. Situations Leading To Foreclosure - 19
3. Contingencies Taking Towards Foreclosure - 24
4. Parties Involved In Foreclosure - 28
5. Relationship between Tax Lien and Foreclosure - 31
6. The Foreclosure Period - 36
7. Importance Of Having An Idea About The Time Period Of Foreclosure - 41
8. Smart Facts To Keep Foreclosure Away - 44
9. Be Smart And Avoid Foreclosures - 47
10. Don't Ignore The Situation - 53
11. Planning Your Assets - 57
12. Making Smart Money - 61
13. Identify Your Issues - 65
14. Conclusions About Foreclosure - 68

CHAPTER II: Short Sale

1. Short Sale - 81
2. Short Sale Basics - 90
3. A Look At The Short Sale Process - 95
4. Finding The Perfect Short Sale Opportunity - 103
5. Negotiating With Short Sale Sellers - 115
6. The Short Sale Document Package - 133
7. Short Sale Investors - 146
8. Lender Negotiations - 156
9. Real Estate Agent Negotiations - 167
10. Due Diligence - 173
11. Making Sure The Price Is Right - 182
12. Dealing With Fixer Uppers - 192
13. Staging For Faster Sales - 202
14. Going For The Exit - 211
15. The Bottom Line Advantage - 216
16. To Sell Or Not To Sell - 221
17. Conclusions About Short Sale - 235

INTRODUCTION

*F*oreclosure

In the recent times, the concept of foreclosure has become immensely popular. In spite of the gaining popularity, there are many people who do not know about the reasons and circumstances that show the way to Foreclosures. Not only that, but people do not even know how to avoid foreclosures. One has to have in-depth knowledge of the facts related to the foreclosures.

This will give a better understanding and help people to handle situations. Like what are foreclosures? Situations leading to foreclosures, the laws related to the homeowners and money lenders, procedures to know of when one is involved in a foreclosure and more.

This is a book which will help one in understanding the different minute details involved in foreclosures and how one can avoid the same. Read on for some interesting and basic facts on foreclosure! The real estate market has suffered a set back right from the year 2006. Since then the home owners around the globe have been forced to come to terms with foreclosures.

A foreclosure is a term associated with forgoes or fail to retain the ownership rights of one's house or property. Failing to pay for the mortgage of the purchased property leads to foreclosures. Believe it or not the present economic slump is also a powerful effect of the foreclosures that have been happening over a period of time.

Short Sale

If you've been following the real estate market at all with an eye toward getting in, you probably have heard that short sales are a hot way to get in and make a lot of cash in the process. While they were once a rarity, short sales are now a common tool used by lenders to get rid of proprieties with bad debt loans on them.

This type of purchase takes advantage of an old adage that a penny saved is a penny earned. In this case, however, the pennies saved are those a mortgage lender is trying to recover to your potential benefit! There are a lot of old adages that apply to real estate investing. Smart investors take many of these to heart. For example, striking while the iron is hot in this market can net buyers some incredible deals that can translate to very big earnings down the road. This can even translate into near instant returns on investment if a buyer plays the right cards. But, since it's also true that money doesn't always come (extremely) easy, if it's your intention to make a bundle in the short sale market, you will have to do a little work.

When the potential profits are explored, however, the elbow grease won't seem all that bad. Whether you are interested in short sales or not, the truth is the best time to buy with an eye toward investment is when the market is down. This means that prices will be, as well. The best way to buy property and take full advantage of reduced prices if often found in the short sale. This unique selling mode is one that gives investors an ability to purchase property at a fraction of its value so lenders can at least get a little return on their own investment and save themselves the trouble of having to manage property in an inventory that is likely already too large and cumbersome to handle.

Short sales are basically a compromise or discounted price. When owners can no longer pay the mortgage, but a full-priced resale doesn't look feasible in a timely fashion, banks will explore this option. Short sales help the original owners by ridding them of the property in question before a foreclosure goes on their records. They also help lending institutions by helping them get some of their money back from the original investment. Purchasing property in a short sale circumstance is a bit different than other types of buying. Investors need to know the ropes and how to take advantage of the pricing to earn rather nice returns.

Once a property has been purchased, they will also need to know how to assess what needs to be done to turn the buy around quickly and at a profit. In this book, we will discuss why short sales can benefit you – the investor. We will also take a close look at the process of buying, how to prepare a property for resale and what to expect in regard to returns. Getting into the short sale market is a little different than buying a house outright for what is owed on the loan or at a price closer to the value.

The process can be longer and even a little more arduous, but the end result is often a solid purchase at a fraction of the value. If you want to make serious cash with foreclosure short sales, you will find buying a discount does give you a big financial advantage going into a deal. It doesn't, however, remove the need to give due diligence in advance and after purchases. The more research you do in advance of a purchase, the more likely you are to make decent or even excellent returns down the road. While a short sale will give you "instant equity" in a purchase, it isn't a guarantee of a big return all on its own. You will have to property prepare, price and market a home for faster resale.

There are secrets to buying good properties at low prices and turning them around for a profit – even in this market. Short sales are the best place to start. If you want to make money in this market, striking while the iron is hot can pay off. Just keep another old saying in mind: Buyer beware! The more you know about a property before you buy, the better off you will be. Stay on your toes and you can make a good profit in this volatile market.

CHAPTER I

FORECLOSURE

"Observe, listen and learn. You cannot know everything. Anyone who thinks they know everything is destined for mediocrity".

-. Donald Trump (Businessman + Pte. USA 96-20)

FORECLOSURE

Foreclosure is technically defined as a right of redemption on a property. The situation arises when a person has taken a loan on property by mortgaging it or has purchased the property through a loan and is not being able to pay for the repayment installments. In most cases the borrower is a house owner who had accrued his property with the aid of loans, which due to some reason he is unable to pay back in time. As soon as the borrower fails to pay the loan amount he or she becomes a "defaulter". If the defaulter has no other source to pay off for the loan, the property is seized and sold to recover the loan amount. This will result in a decrease in credit rating for the borrower who becomes a looser in the future.

A borrower can take a loan for purchase of the property from a financial institution or a bank. The sanction of the loan involves quite a few legal formalities. This results in the intervention of a third party in the cases. At this point, the judicial and non judicial foreclosures come into the picture. Judicial foreclosures are foreclosures that are overlooked and executed by the court. In this case the lender can take over the property directly with the assistance of court intervention. The process would be conducted by the mortgagee or the agent under the guidance and surveillance of the court.

The final decision is taken by the mortgagee or lender in case of non judicial foreclosures. The foreclosure would be conducted all the way through by a public auction system. The borrower receives a notice from the sheriff in case of judicial foreclosure. The auction is conducted at the court hall. The process involves legal formalities held between the lender and the borrower. A person who is purchasing a property in an auction can make huge profits, if he can manage to buy the property at a lesser auctioned price than that of its market value. In cases where the bank takes over the property one would have to wait till the bank finds a perfect buyer for the same.

Given the facts, it can be wisely said that Foreclosures certainly aid borrowers to meet their loan arrears. Owners of a property try to avoid the lengthy and elaborate procedures involved in 5 Foreclosures. This is specially related to borrowers who have a history of bad credit because it will be very difficulty for them to avail loans. Though there are institutions to assist you with foreclosures yet for the interest rate can turn out to be sky high for borrowers with a bad credit history. One can purchase a relatively high priced property at a low cost at foreclosure auctions or sale. This is seen as an advantage for the buyers. The purchaser of the foreclosed property can then sell off the same at a profit making and titanic gains!

"Winners are not afraid of losing, losers are. Failure is part of the process of success. People who avoid failure also avoid success".

-. Robert Kiyosaki (Author)

SITUATIONS LEADING TO FORECLOSURES

When no further monetary dealings are possible between the borrower and the lender, proceedings for Foreclosures commences. When borrower is entirely bankrupt, he can find no alternative to repay the loans he had taken for his or against his property. Then, he is left with no other choice apart from the Foreclosure. Foreclosures do not give anyone the consent to throw you out of the house without prior notice. Only when there is judicial intervention, the court can order you to leave your house. The court too has a set of rules for foreclosures and evictions which must be followed.

When the foreclosure of your property is handled by a bank, it is recommended for you to find out from the bank as to when they will begin the procedures for the same. It may as long as 90 days for the bank to commence with the proceedings. It is best to have the knowledge of the dates of proceedings, so that you can make alternative arrangements to move out in that span of time. This is because you will have to find a house which you like and fits within your rent budget and then move out your belongings. Foreclosure proceedings begin when a borrower skips the mortgage and all other associated payments related to the owned property.

A bank will first try and work out a solution with the borrower so that the foreclosure can be avoided. Banks are known to make settlements or find alternative methods prior to the decision of the foreclosure. When the borrower continues to miss the payments and avoids contact, the bank will resort to legal action. It will first send a note to the borrower demanding payment, based on the acceleration clause.

The acceleration clause is a kind of mortgage note. It reads that upon failure to make the repayments the total amount which is due on the 6 borrower will have to be paid in total at call. It would also include the amount of interest calculated by the bank as per the terms of the contract.

Once you receive the mortgage note from the bank, it is indication enough that you should contact your attorney. An attorney will help you to proceed with your legal formalities regarding the foreclosure. A mortgage note is the starting point of a future foreclosure. The banks would follow up by sending across the "Notice of Intent to foreclose" the notice is served with the help of the sheriff and the court. Once the notice is served it is expected from the borrower to meet up with the authorities and work out a solution. When the borrower does not respond to any notice or call the borrower will be tagged guilt of missing payments by the court.

The court will apparently give legal permission to the bank to then begin the proceedings of foreclosure. The bank then announces the foreclosure of the property in the local media through advertisement. An auction is followed on the decided date and the property is handed to the highest bidder. The borrower loses his property as the price for his loan.

"Your greatness is limited only by the investments you make in yourself."

-. Grant Cardone (Businessman + Author)

CONTINGENCIES TAKING TOWARDS FORECLOSURE

When a borrower misses to make repayments for his amount of loan, it will lead to foreclosure of the property. The specified number of missed payments which would lead to seal on the borrower's property is mentioned in the loan contract. The number of defaulted payments also depends on the characteristics of loan you have along with the contract terms.

The mortgage contract states clearly as to how many payments you can miss ahead of a Notice of Default is filed against you. As and when a person misses the first payment of the loan, it is a big indication that in the future there could be a situation of foreclosure. A home equity credit line to lock your interest rates must be set to prevent such a situation.

This will give you the prospect to get fast cash in cases of emergency. Missing paying up a mortgage payment not as simple as missing a credit card payment. It could be counted similar to a criminal offence. After you have missed a maximum of four mortgage payments, you can be assured that a Foreclosure proceeding would be started against you. The credit history of a person is negatively affected when he evades a mortgage repayment.

A bad credit history reduces the chances of getting future loans. These loans could be useful to a person as he can save his house from getting mortgaged, through the loans. If you default at the mortgage repayments, chances of your getting future loans decrease with every payments default. Avoid missing payments in a row as this will speed up the foreclosure procedure for you. Once you have missed around three to four payments, the lender party, bank or financial institution will begin the foreclosure proceedings against you.

"Don't compare yourself to anyone in this world, if you do, you are insulting yourself".

-. Bill gates (Microsoft)

PARTIES INVOLVED IN FORECLOSURE

Missed payments would lead the banks or the financial institutions to declare foreclosure. Once the foreclosure has been declared the rest would follow:

- Mortgage holders and other lien holders who hold interest in loans on your property, used as collateral, would be amongst one of the first people to foreclose your property.

- Banks and additional financial institutions from where you had got a lump sum loan for your property following which you failed to pay them back the monthly installments are also liable to put up your property for a foreclosure. This will be done with assistance from the local court or judiciary.

- A forced foreclosure and eviction can be issued by the sheriff, if the homeowner fails to make the payments even after repeated warnings. Notice is even served when the borrower does not respond or ignores eviction notices.

- The property is finally foreclosed by the auction houses. Once a foreclosure has been declared, legal notices are put up in public stating the details of the property in auction. This would begin within 90 days after you have failed to make your mortgage payments and your property has been declared for foreclosures.

"If you are prepared and you know what you will do, it is not a risk. You have to figure out how to get there. There is always a way to get there. "

-. **Mark Cuban (Dallas Mavericks Owner)**

RELATION BETWEEN TAX LIEN AND FORECLOSURE

A tax lien is imposed on a person once the property has been decided for foreclosure. A tax lien is a type of tax imposed on property by legal institutions to secure payments of the respective taxes. These could be taxes that have been imposed on real or personal property that are a result of one failing to pay income tax or other associated taxes.

In case of Foreclosures tax liens are generally imposed upon real estates that the property owner has to pay up under all circumstances.

This tax is even imposed upon the current property owner if it was actually incurred by the prior owner of the property. There are various methods by which tax lien related payments could be made.

A property owner has the rights to make these payments directly or has the option to utilize the services of a mortgage holder via an escrow account.

In case of the property owner using the services of a mortgage company, the company is liable to receive all notices related to the property and its payments and even if the property owner does not possess an escrow account, the mortgage company is bound to pay up the same in his or her behalf.

However, you they have every right to demand the same from their client. In some cases the mortgage company can go as far as creating an escrow account for their clients so that they can make their payments through the same. If this is not done the mortgage company might end up making a loss in its value of mortgage lien if the taxing agency sold out the property to meet unpaid taxes foreclosure.

In cases where the property owner sells off his property before foreclosure with government aid, the tax lien if any is paid off during the closing of deal from the sale proceeds.

Tax lien comes into focus when it is not paid prior to foreclosures. In such a situation the property could be seized off and sold at a foreclosure.

For a purchaser, it becomes obligatory to check on a property that he plans to purchase especially if via foreclosures. This is to verify and check for any associated tax liens, unless he wants to fall into numerous legal clichés associated with the same. Further he will end up paying tax liens for expenses he has not incurred. He will have to pay because he purchased a property where the previous owner was a tax defaulter.In case of personal properties it becomes mandatory for the present owner to pay up all related taxes. A owner will not be permitted to sell his property unless all property related taxes have been paid by him.

Every government ensures that property taxes are paid by property owners. This saves them from a tax lien being issued against them. However, real estate owners are big time gainers when it comes to tax liens.

The real estate boom that happened in recent years is in fact a result of tax liens. Properties at prime locations whose owners had failed to pay up the property taxes due to some financial crisis or personal problems led to the boom. The real estate developers who generally have a lot of money in hand make an offer to the property owners to buy property and pays off all his tax liens.

This makes them the owners of prime properties at strategic locations which they can later sell at a much elevated price. All they have to do is list out such properties with tax lapse, from which they can churn out whale profits.

"Life is too short to surround yourself with people who do not contribute anything to your life".

-. Jeff Bezos (Amazon)

THE FORECLOSURE PERIOD

Would you like to know the amount of time required in the entire process of foreclosure? Well, this is one question that pops up in the minds of all owners involved in foreclosure. Property owners panic as to how long it will be for them from the time they take delivery of a foreclosure notice from the sheriff to the auctions to happen, and the property deal to be closed.

Since they do not have the proper idea of the foreclosure period, they cannot take adequate measures to stop the property being foreclosed or chalk out other alternative plans.

Factors affecting foreclosure time period: The duration of a foreclosure depends largely upon the governing body or state and its legal laws. The prevalent law is a vital factor that would decide when the foreclosure proceedings would start and end. This begins once the property owner has missed a mortgage payment. The property owner whose property is to be foreclosed must be aware of the same so that they are well equipped to face the situation.

Estimating time frame:

- Mortgage companies: they would generally begin the foreclosure process 3- 6 months post the owner misses the first mortgage payment.

- Though the stated period is 30 days after first missed payment, most money lenders are kind enough to provide property owners a second chance. The lenders give the owners 3-6 months time in hand to make necessary arrangements. If the loan default is paid within that period, the question of foreclosure does not come into the picture.

- Constant touch with banks: If you are a smart property owner who has fallen into a foreclosure situation, you can delay the entire foreclosure process. This can be done by 12 being in constant contact with your bank or financial institution.

This would lengthen the foreclosure procedure by months if you manage to keep your bank occupied with various paper work related to foreclosure or even make an attempt at resolving the foreclosure sale. You can even ask your bank for extra time if you see some money coming in the future. By avoiding regular contact with the bank one would only speed up the foreclosure sale as the bank would assume that you are avoiding making of any payments.

The actual eviction from the property would only occur after the sheriff sale is over. This happens after the bank has secured a court order for eviction. This could take months to take place at times. This is to give the homeowners adequate time to relocate and plan their future. In extreme fortunate cases they can aim at refinancing or repaying their loans.

- The actual foreclosure sale would only happen two to three weeks or even months after the sheriff has declared and passed a notice. The sale of property would occur at a county courthouse which is attended by the owner too.

"When I was little, my parents used to get mad at me because I kept asking them and questioning everything they answered me. I did not believe many things they said and forced them to justify all their answers until I saw a sense in them".

-. Ellon Musk (Tesla + Paypal)

IMPORTANCE OF HAVING AN IDEA ABOUT THE TIME PERIOD OF FORECLOSURE

Most property owners who are involved in a property dispute are unaware of the exact time that they would be involved in a case their property is put up for foreclosure sale.

Since they do not have the idea of the time frame, they cannot plan any last minute actions to save their property from the foreclosure and sale. Moreover, when the sheriff plans to take quick action, the owner and family could be thrown out of the hose before they could even contemplate it.

This will just a make a person understand, how important it is to know about the time period involved in the foreclosure process. You can meet up your lawyer during that period and avoid the foreclosure by devising a plan and payments scheme.

"I never think about the future, it comes too soon. You have to learn to live in the moment, if you live worried about the future you will not be able to enjoy the present".

-. Albert Einstein (Scientific)

SMART FACTS TO KEEP FORECLOSURE AWAY

Who would like to loose his property through a foreclosure sale? Not many. It is not everyday that a person makes a house or a property. After all every body have various dreams and aspirations around their owned property. This is the very reason they would not like to simply hand it over to a third party. There may have been some financial crisis or unavoidable circumstances for which the owner may have failed to pay the mortgage loan resulting in a foreclosure.

Ups and downs are a part of life. It is a sorry state of affairs but definitely not the end of the road. Well, you don't have to worry! There are numerous options slowly emerging for property owners. These are like the magic clauses which are adept in order to prevent foreclosure sale of their property. If you have plans to avoid a foreclosure sale of your property, the first step that you ought to take is to contact your financial advisor. a legal firm which is well experienced in handling a foreclosure situation will guide you through the various options available.

Apart from this you can look up different websites on the net for advises or read up blogs of people who have been victims of a foreclosure sale. You will come across some information which will give you the tips to come out of the foreclosure mess. These will give you a reasonable idea on how to advance. As you read on, we will be giving you some interesting tips on how to avoid foreclosures on your property in this chapter.

"I don't think there is any other quality so essential to the success of any person, as the quality of perseverance. It surpasses almost everything, even nature. "

-. John D. Rockefeller (Standard Oil)

BE SMART AND AVOID FORECLOSURES

Below we present a series of steps to follow to help avoid a possible foreclosure;

1. To begin with get in touch with counseling agent to advise you for a home loan modification. A home loan modification will help you reduce your monthly EMI's for home loan. This will help you to retain your house as small monthly payments could be affordable and chances of skipping it will be less.

2. Talk to your money lender to help work out solutions to prevent a foreclosure. Be it your bank or any other financial institution from where you have availed the loan, speak to them for alternative ideas and plans to help you save your house.

If you're unable to make your mortgage payment, get in touch with your lender immediately in order to stop foreclosure. Ignoring the bills will only make matters worse, increasing the likelihood that you'll lose your home for sure.

Borrowers who look for foreclosure help early are much more likely to work out a solution, even in dire situation. Mortgage companies want to avoid foreclosure as much as you; this is because they make more money in the interest involved in the loan than they make in processing a foreclosure a deal. Based on your situation, your lender may be able to offer the foreclosure help that you require.

3. Look for reinstatement opportunities: in this method, the owner of the house who is apparently also the defaulter is given another chance.

He can choose to make the payments on a future date of the entire amount of loans outstanding. Who knows you can suddenly get a bulk amount from company bonus, profit or a tax refund.

4. Go for a forbearance agreement: That is the lender allowing the borrower to decrease or minimize the mortgage payments for a time period. Within this period options for payments are worked out on the current loan.

5. Plan a repayment plan with your funds lender, till you have money structured to pay your actual loan amount. This repayment plan would be so made, so that your monthly payments are made much lower and affordable.

This will help you to make up most of your losses and be in a better financial position. Once you financial position improves you will to be able to pay off your loans at the actual amount once again.

6. Mortgage modification. Mortgage modification is the process of working out an agreement with your money lender, whereby you could request your money lender to change certain terms on your loan document. With the modification you could still pay your monthly loan amount at an affordable rate.

Changes could be brought about by incorporating the amount of the missed payments into the existing loan balance.

Alternatively a change in payment can by modified by altering the interest rates from variable to be fixed. One could also extend the number of years for repaying the loan. Increasing the years would reduce the monthly loan expenditure.

7. Make sure you opt for mortgage insurance. Mortgage insurances are insurances issued against your loan amount which you can use in crisis situations. It can be used in the times of foreclosure whereby you could obtain some amount of money to save the present situation.

An insurance claim can delay your foreclosure for months. You would qualify if your loan is between 4 and 12 months period. All you need to do is sign an interest free promissory note to enable a lien to be imposed upon your property till you are able to pay off the same. These are the numerous advantages of mortgage insurance.

8. Avoid missing a payment if you don't want to fall into the foreclosure trap. It's best to avoid missing a payment.

One of the finest ways to avoid a Foreclosure is to bring to a halt the filing of Notice of Default. The only way to prevent it is to be in constant touch with your money lender and not to stay away from him. Staying in touch can enable you to work out a solution.

Your money lender may opt for forbearance that is by giving you adequate time to reorganize for the current situation and the default payments. In rare cases the lender can give you debt forgiveness, that is, he may forego your current payments for a time period. But it is advisable not to expect this degree of goodness.

Your money lender may also extend your awaiting payments over a large period of time. When you talk to a lender in good faith, he may come up some options which may be beneficial to you. Though you cannot thank the lender enough, but you must try and meet the redesigned and comfortable pay scheme.

"Both if you think you can, or if you think you can't, you are right. Our thoughts determine our success or failure".

-.Henry Ford (Ford Motors)

DON'T IGNORE THE SITUATION

Ignoring will fuel the problem: that could end you up face to face with a foreclosure. Be open to negotiations and conversations with your lender at all times. Your lender would definitely work out an option for you. Contact the State Government Housing Office for help: you can get in touch with the government housing office for any questions and information's that you would want to know regarding foreclosures.

Having sufficient information about foreclosure and its connected laws will give you plenty of chance to plan a way out of this predicament situation. Get in touch with your state housing development counselor at first.

They would be bound to find a way out for you. In the United States of America there exists HUD or the Housing and Urban Development association in every state which help homeowners in times of crisis through free counseling. These counseling sessions throws light on how to avoid foreclosures. The counseling sessions are educative and helpful.

They can go to the extent of explaining you every detailed law associated with foreclosures, help you plan your finance so that you could avoid the same. In some cases, they could also become the intermediary between you and your money lender.

This is best alternative in situations where you would not like to face each other. Make your savings more than the expenditure: When in a crisis situation, spend only on necessities rather than luxuries and other impulse purchases. Try and cut down your everyday expenditure so that you could make your mortgage payments.

When you have to make a choice between the credit card and the mortgage payment, pay for your mortgage. Remember, credit card are unsecured loans and can be settled by paying a lower price later.

Cut down on restaurants, movies, outings and vacations for a time till you have made up for your losses.

"Luck is a sweat dividend. The more you sweat, the luckier you will be".

-. Ray Kroc (McDonalds)

PLANNING YOUR ASSETS

A foreclosure can be avoided if you have worked through your years to build your assets. Assets could be in the form of a car, gold or silver jewelry. Assets with high resale values, any policies, shares or savings could be used at this point of time to make your mortgage payment and save your house.

Like for Christmas you could buy a policy apart from your spree shopping, for your birthday you could make some investments. All these little savings are big help when you are in a financial mess. Take up freelancing part time jobs. If you can add an extra income by doing a part time job to meet your mortgage payment take it up! After all an extra effort can lead to an extra income that can help you avoid a foreclosure.

You will, be able to save your asset with a little hard work and that too for a limited period of time.

Foreclosure consultants empty promises trap: the foreclosure consultant who go outright to demonstrate to you that a foreclosure could be preventable if you remunerated them a certain amount of money. Be smart and smell the foul play. Instead utilize that cash to pay back your mortgage loans.

In fact at worst cases you could end up being a part of a foreclosure scam. These are scams that generate from profit making organizations which lure or convince you that they would avoid a foreclosure for you.

No miracles happen as you see the foreclosure in front of your eyes but they are successful in extracting a heavy amount of money.

One could avoid a foreclosure when he files for a bankruptcy. This would with held foreclosure proceedings for a time period. One can make the most of this time by planning out an option as to how he will meet the loan repayment situation of the mortgage.

Take help from an attorney. If you are a novice in this it would be best for you to recruit a foreclosure attorney. The attorney will direct you on how to avoid a foreclosure. He will give you the best options available to and will also come to your help with all the essential paper work necessary. Read on the internet for various blogs and advices on how to stop a foreclosure sale.

I am sure these will be helpful. You can get an occasion to relate with people who have experienced or are about to experience a foreclosure deal. There is absolutely nothing that you cannot find on the internet. The best advice on foreclosure along 19 with practical examples will be available for you to read and understand. You can then try and imply it in your practical scenario. Use the search engines for all the help that you need.

"Build your reputation carefully".

-. Ivanka Trump (Businesswoman)

MAKING SMART MONEY

Make smart money lender choice: One of the most important factors that could help one avoid a foreclosure is to study your money lender before you pick him or her. Not only that, but it is equally important to understand all the minute details of a loan prior to accepting it.

There is no limit to options available to stay away from a foreclosure. Abundant options can be worked out. Your alternatives don't stop unless you have given up the fight. So it is very important to be strong minded. You have to work towards a solution.

Remember all the happiness you felt when you finally became the owner of the property. Think of the good times that you have spent there and those uncountable memories.

All of it will give you the strength to carry on your fight to save your property. Mind the use of credit cards: You will realize that after a time you are unable to pay your mortgages because you had been busy paying off your credit card bills. Activate home equity lines: At least 90% of foreclosures could be prohibited or delayed if home equity lines of credit were previously activated. This can often be set up for no cost and can lock in rates as low as 4%. In most cases you pay zero each month if you do not access the line.

No one ever expects sudden health problems, loss of a job or emergency requiring funds fast. All of these are contingencies. These events might prevent obtaining a loan once they occur. By setting up a home equity credit line before you ever miss a mortgage payment, you will have money when you really need it.

Just write yourself a check. When things get back in order, pay back the line and then use it again the next time. But do not take advantage of it and make regular useless expenditures. It is there for times of emergencies to bail you out of financial crisis.

A friend in need is a friend indeed. In this crisis period do not forget to take help from a friend who might help you out with the money required to meet your mortgage payments.

After all you can always pay a friend back that too without an interest when your sunny days arrive again! And you would not have to loose your house to a foreclosure! Do not feel ashamed to ask help from a friend, relative or close associate. After all if they really love you they would never allow you to loose your home to a disastrous thing as a foreclosure. In case you have a big ego, crush it my dear or it will crush your property.

"For to win one hundred victories in one hundred battles is not the acme of skill. To subdue the enemy without fighting is the acme of skill".

-. **Sun Tzu (Chinese General)**

IDENTIFY YOUR ISSUES

Face your problems: share your problems with your friends and associates and with your entire money lender. They will definitely find a solution for you. It is wise to accept that there is a problem rather than run away from it and thinking all is fine. Look for genuine money lenders: some money lender will show you no other alternative apart from the foreclosure.

They are the clan of lenders who are there only to make money and do not believe in humanitarian grounds. Remember options in 90% cases are workable so always take multiple opinions and consultations before you take a decision or are forced to take one. Sell your property.

You can yourself sell your property if you want to avoid a foreclosure. It works! Selling your home yourself will get you a higher amount rather than selling your house off through foreclosure at an auction.

This way you will definitely get more money from the sale proceeds with which you can purchase a lower or equivalent value property without having to loose out on a whole lot of money and engaging yourself in numerous paper work related to foreclosures.

You can good money for your house and be saved from any sticky embarrassing situation related to foreclosure. The last resort: even if you have lost your house or property to foreclosure you still have an option to buy it back even after you are evicted!

You can end up being the highest bidder if you are able to organize the cash required to purchase your property under auction during the period when the sheriff plans your foreclosure and entire eviction process. If money is arranged prior to the auction you can buy it, but do not pay an amount which costs you more than the property.

Buy a new one!

"Outstanding leaders go out of their way to boost the self-esteem of their personnel. If people believe in themselves, it's amazing what they can accomplish".

-. Sam Walton (Walmart)

CONCLUSION ABOUT FORECLOSURE

Foreclosures are painful for the owners of property.

There are times in life when hardships fall on us and losing property as a result of it is saddening. Life can never be foreseen but contingencies are inevitable. It is thus recommended to save for the hard times. Foreclosure is a just another loss and can be avoided if life is well planned and money is intelligently spend!

Homeowners Options to Avoid Foreclosure

If you are looking to profit from the poor real estate market and the large number of foreclosed homes across the country, there is one important thing you must know. You do not need to wait until foreclosure proceedings start. Yes, you can get amazing deals on foreclosed properties, but there are other options too. These include foreclosure short sales and deeply discounted for sale by owner properties.

Foreclosure short sales occur when the homeowners or current home occupants cannot pay their mortgage. There is no foreseeable solution in the near future. They will lose their home. It is honestly just a matter of when. To save their credit score and to avoid costly and lengthy foreclosure proceedings for the mortgage lender, a short sale is decided on.

The mortgage lender agrees to sell for less than the outstanding mortgage debt. The lender will take a loss, but they still get some of their money and avoid foreclosure proceedings.

For sale by owner sales are often last minute attempts to avoid foreclosure by the delinquent borrower alone. Sometimes, the mortgage lender refused a short sale.

Unfortunately, it isn't always easy to find soon-to-be foreclosed homes for sale. In some cases, they are risky.

You need to target homeowners who have reached the point of no return. There are many steps for homeowners to avoid foreclosure. You need to familiarize yourself with these steps to save yourself time.

Loan reinstatement. With today's economy, many individuals are finding themselves in the unemployment line. In some areas of the United States, it is difficult to find a job. It can take a year or more. In other areas, an unemployed person can find a job and be working in as little as a few weeks or months. Don't avoid, but proceed with caution with individuals who are only facing temporary hardships.

When dealing with for sale by owner homes, the owner can change their mind at any time before the final closing. If the current home occupant finds employment or gets their mortgage lender to work with them during these tough, but temporary times, you may be left out in the cold.

Loan modification. This shouldn't be a major issue for you as a potential homebuyer. Most homeowners approach lenders with this option right from the start. A loan modification involves readjusting the interest rate, the monthly payments, or the overall term of the loan.

Many homeowners, unless unemployed, can save their homes from foreclosure with loan modifications. If you want to do a good deed, offer the suggestion. If you want to make a profit, keep this to yourself. After all, the homeowner should already know about loan modifications. If not, it is their loss and your gain.

Foreclosure short sales. As previously stated, the decision to short sell is made by the mortgage lender and in agreement with the current homeowner or occupants. This is considered a last ditch attempt to avoid foreclosure. In most cases, short sales are a great way to profit from the real estate market.

You must proceed with caution though, if a new homeowner just acquired a mortgage within the last year, they owe a significant amount on their mortgage. Always compare the home's appraised value with the short sale selling price. Homes can depreciate. Remember your goal is to get a good deal and possibly resell for a profit.

For sale by owner properties. As with foreclosure short sales, proceed with caution with for sale by owner properties. You will always find homeowners who want to turn a profit. This means selling a home for more than it is worth. If you know the home is near foreclosure, use this as a bargaining tool.

Those who are truly interested in avoiding foreclosure and protecting their credit will sell the home at a fair price. Aim for the outstanding amount on their mortgage, plus a small amount for first and last months rent at a new apartment.

As you can see, there are ways that a homeowner can avoid foreclosure.

Use these steps to your advantage. Save time and money by opting for those who have reached the point of no return. If they don't sell their home, foreclosure right around the corner.

Landlords: 5 Reasons to Examine Foreclosure Sales

If you own and rent just one piece of property you are consider a landlord. Property owners have the potential to make money and a lot of it, especially when the right cards are played. Are you making money now from your rental properties? Would you like to make more? You can with foreclosure short sales.

Short sales are an alternative to foreclosure. The decision to offer the property in the form of a short sale is made by both the borrower and the lender. Everyone needs to be in agreement because less than the outstanding mortgage amount is sought. For example, if a borrower owes $20,000 on a $45,000 home, the property may be listed for sale at $15,000.

Some lenders try to get as much of their money as possible, while others want to unload the property as quickly as possible. This means there is always the potential to make money.

So, why should you, as a landlord, closely examine foreclosure short sales?

1 – Wide Range of Properties to Choose From

The poor economy has everyone in a pinch. With a high rate of unemployment and a troubling economy, many homeowners are unable to make their mortgage payments. Soon their debt is spinning out of control.

Right now, you may be running a profitable rental business, but not all landlords are. Due to non-paying tenants, empty units, and poor financial choices, some landlords are finding themselves in or nearing foreclosure.

This means you will find a wide range of properties for sale in the pre foreclosure stages, often available as short sale properties. All of these properties, including single-family homes, can be purchased, renovated, and rented.

2 – Get a Good Deal

As previously stated, short sales are alternatives to foreclosure. They involve selling a property for less than the outstanding mortgage amount due. Why do borrowers and lenders agree to short sales? Because it is much better than foreclosure.

Borrowers do not suffer damaging consequences to their credit and most are able to avoid bankruptcy. Mortgage lenders get their money faster, even though they do accept a lower amount. They also avoid lengthy and costly foreclosure proceedings.

Since both mortgage lenders and borrowers are willing to accept less money for the home, there is the potential to get a good deal. By looking in the right places and bargaining with all lenders directly, you can get an amazing deal on any type of property.

Foreclosure short sales often result in a good deal, but always proceed with caution. Homes do depreciate in value in a poor market. Ensure the short sale price is significantly below the home's appraised value.

3 – Easy to Turn a Profit

Most buyers of foreclosure short sale properties are first time homeowners or investors. These investors buy a home and resell it. You do have this option, but use your experience as a landlord to make a profit. Consider the long-term aspect. By finding a low-priced short sale property, you can turn a profit in no time at all. For example, if you are able to purchase a 2-family home for $20,000 and rent out those two rental units for $800 a month each, the rental units pay for themselves in just 13 months. After that, you profit.

4 – Easy Way to Expand Rental Properties

If you are a successful landlord who is already making a profit or in good financial standing due to your rental properties, you may want more. Unfortunately, the poor real estate market makes that difficult. Many homeowners try to sell their home as soon as they notice a problem. They know that foreclosure may be months away. Unfortunately, most of these property owners have unrealistic expectations. They not only want to get out from their current mortgage, but make a profit. In most cases, that will not happen. You and all buyers know, the less you spend the more money you make.

For landlords, foreclosure short sales are an easy and affordable way to expand a rental property business.

5 – Bargaining Power

If you are like most Americans, you may need financing to purchase a short sale property. Since you are an established landlord, you are at an advantage. Not only should you have decent credit and adequate cash flow, but you have bargaining power. Not only approach lenders about buying a short sale property, but financing the mortgage directly through them! This is a win win situation. Sell yourself. You have experience buying properties, making repairs, finding quality tenants, and paying your bills on time. Remember, mortgage lenders want to avoid foreclosure proceedings at all costs. This leaves you with the power to bargain.

CHAPTER II

SHORT-SALE

"You only have to do a very few things right in your life so long as you don't do too many things wrong".

-. Warren Buffet (Berkshire Hathaway)

SHORT SALE

You have probably heard this term used frequently lately and have no idea what it means. A short sale is a type of real estate investment that flourishes in a down market. Right now, most of the United States is in what is known as a buyer's market. This means that there are more homes on the market for sale than there are buyers. When supply exceeds demand, the prices drop.

This is not the case in all areas of the United States. In some still coveted areas, the supply of home has not exceeded the demand and the housing values have stayed the same or even appreciated.

For the most part, however, the residential real estate market has crashed. States such as Florida, California and Nevada have an influx of foreclosures.

In many areas of Florida, short sales are the normal financial transaction for a real estate closing.

Many people are under the misconception that a short sale is only something that can only take place when someone is entering into foreclosure. It is important to realize that not all short sales are foreclosures or close to being foreclosed upon. There is another misconception that you have to pay cash if you are buying a short sale property. Again, this is false information.

You can finance a short sale property, but you have to be ready to buy the home in a short amount of time. In other words, there 5 can be no financing contingencies on the real estate contract. And you will have to show proof that you are able to make this purchase either with cash or with approved financing.

Some people think that all short sales occur in blighted areas. Again, not true. As a matter of fact, most short sales in some states are in upscale neighborhoods. Short sales are all different. Each person who is seeking to sell their home and is willing to go for the short sale deal has a unique situation.

There is one constant with all short sales, however. This is that all of the owners of the property owe more money on the property than the property is worth. This is the constant and what makes them a short sale client.

This book will teach you not only how to find short sale clients, but also how you can negotiate with them, different financing options, how to get partners to invest, what type of documents you need to facilitate the short sale and even title issues that you should be aware of before you purchase a house "as is." Everything that you need to know about a short sale is found right here in one book. So, sit back and relax and get ready to learn everything you ever wanted to know about the short sale.

So, What Is A Short Sale?

The short sale normally occurs when a homeowner is about to go into foreclosure. They may be desperate to sell their homes and are doing everything that they can do to get rid of the home. They actually owe more money on the house than the house is worth and are anticipating having to bring a check to the closing. This is not something that they want to do, but nor do they want to go through the trauma of foreclosure.

A foreclosure occurs when a mortgage company comes in and takes a house back from a borrower who has defaulted on his or her mortgage. The default is usually the case of them not paying their mortgage payment.

Generally, mortgage company will begin foreclosure proceedings after a borrower has not paid their mortgage for two months. Prior to the foreclosure, the homeowner has a chance to stave off the proceedings. They can, and usually do, try to work things out with the mortgage.

The mortgage company will usually work with homeowners who may be facing tough times due to losing a job or some other catastrophic event, such as illness. In some cases, the mortgage company will suspend payments for a couple of months or ask that the borrower only pay interest. Sometimes this works to pull a borrower out of trouble, but it is usually stalling the inevitable.

The lender will stave off the short sale if the property is on the market. This may be able to buy a borrower a bit more time so that they can sell the house. In order for the short sale to work, the owner of the property has to be willing to walk away from the deal without any money.

They will not be taking a check with them to the closing nor will they be getting a check from the closing. They will simply hand over the deed and the keys and the house will belong to the short sale investor. This is the only way for a true short sale to work.

Why would any homeowner allow this to happen? Because they owe more on their property than what the property is worth. There are a variety of different reasons why this can happen.

They are as follows:

- They purchased a home during the boom and the house actually depreciated in value

- They have been behind in their mortgage payments and the loan is now backwards

- They have refinanced and borrowed against their equity to the point where there is not more equity

When this occurs, the borrower often finds that they owe way more than the home is worth. The instinct is to just let the bank take it, but many borrowers do not want to go through the trauma of foreclosure and do not want to see this on their credit history.

A foreclosure takes a big hit on the credit history of anyone who goes through it. It is much easier if you can sell the house by conveying it with a deed than having the bank take it. Your credit history will still reflect that you were behind on your mortgage, but the loan will be written off thanks to the negotiating powers of the short sale representative.

The short sale investor finds the owner of the home in a state where he or she is very eager to sell and is willing to walk away without receiving a check. He or she also eager to walk away without having to sink any more money into the house.

The owner of the property that is being sold in the short sale really just wants to walk away an not have to worry about the home any longer. But they do not want to deal with the foreclosure process.

The short sale investor will purchase the house just in the nick of time. He or she will have all of the proper documents and will be able to work with both the lender and the owner of the property in order to get them to agree on a price. The short sale investor gets a house that is worth a lot more than what they paid for it. The original owner of the home gets to walk away from the house and convey it to the short sale investor by deed, instead of going through an embarrassing court proceeding that will entail a foreclosure and will destroy their credit. The lender is happy because they do not have to go through the foreclosure process that will be more expensive than any deal they will make with the short sale investor.

In general, if the short sale goes off without a hitch, everyone will benefit. But in order for a short sale investor to properly work on their negotiations, they will need to know everything that there is to know about short sales. Learn as much as you can about the process so that you can make a better impression on the lender and be able to make a good negotiating deal. The first thing you need to know, once you are ready to begin with the short sale process is to find the perfect short sale vehicle.

"If you ask an economist what's driven economic growth, it's been major advances in things that mattered - the mechanization of farming, mass manufacturing, things like that. The problem is, our society is not organized around doing that".

-. **Larry Page (Google)**

SHORT SALE BASICS

In days gone by, short sales were almost unheard of.

The biggest discount buyers could get was in finding deals in pre-foreclosure or after foreclosure. While price savings are decent in this type of buying, the high potential profits of short sales are just not present. In both of these circumstances, the homeowner (in the case of a pre-foreclosure sale) would try to get as much out of the property price as possible or the bank would after foreclosing.

The idea behind both is to recover at least the amount of the outstanding, unpaid loan. Short sales provide much deeper price cuts. In this circumstance, the bank has already agreed to take less than what the homeowner still owes. The homeowner has agreed to walk away and let the bank recoup as much of its loss as possible. The bank won't get all of its money. The buyer will walk away with nothing – not even a dime.

While this might seem like a lose-lose situation for banks and borrowers, it does have some advantages. Plus, it is has the potential to be a big win situation for you, the investor. Although short sales were once rare, this is no longer so. Now that the subprime lending crisis has turned real estate on its head, more and more lenders are looking at this as a viable option to rid themselves of properties.

This is excellent news for you! Short sales might not be a bank's preferred method for disposing of property on the books, but they are an effective way to do so. In this type of sale, the lending institution accepts less money than is owed by the original buyer for the deed to the property.

The reasons they do so include:

- To give themselves a way to rid bad debts from their books

- To enable them to recover as much of their loss as possible in a more timely fashion than foreclosure

- To avoid the hassles and expenses of the foreclosure process.

While a short sale might not be ideal in a lender's eye, the process is becoming more accepted and widely used. With foreclosure numbers that have been soaring, short sales provide a way to staunch the flow of total losses on a bank's books.

Taking advantage of short sales used to require a lot of work on the part of buyers. First, they had to find properties in the midst of foreclosure and strike immediately to begin negotiating with a bank. Secondly, they had to figure out how to locate a particular bank's loss mitigation department to begin the process of buying. In many cases, short sale offers were turned down flat. Banks knew if they waited they could recover more of their losses and perhaps even walk away with a small profit during a pre-foreclosure sale or even at auction.

Today, banks don't have the luxury of turning down legitimate offers. The times have changed and they are bad for banks, but great for investors. Largely due to the subprime crisis of 2008 many banks are much more agreeable to short sales. Some are even offering this option directly to their clients as a way to avoid the rigors and stresses of foreclosure. When this is the case, short sales can be listed as such directly with a real estate agent.

This is good news for you, the buyer, since direct listings can save you a lot of time and trouble and still net an incredible deal. When a bank has already accepted the idea of selling a property at a short sale price, much of the work is already done. The lender will already have a figure in place that it will accept and the borrower will be poised and ready to sell to get out from underneath the loan. In many cases, finding short sale properties today takes much less work than in the past. The process can still be a little tricky to follow unless a bank has taken a preemptive strike to allow listing. If this is the case, short sales can flow as smoothly as any other potential purchase, or almost as smoothly.

"Strength does not come from winning. Your struggles develop your strengths. When you go through hardships and decide not to surrender, that is strength".

-. **Arnold Schwarzenegger (Actor)**

A LOOK AT THE SHORT SALE PROCESS

Buying a home through the short sale process is not an exact science. Each lender may have specific rules they play by. Still, there are some common steps that go along with the process. When you're dealing in a short sale buy, there are two main types of situations you can run into.

The first will require a little more work. It involves finding your own potential purchase by looking at impending foreclosures. In this case, you'll have to initiate the short sale process. The second buying option involves dealing with a homeowner and a lending institution that have already geared up for the short sale process. In terms of difficulty, the former will require more elbow grease.

STARTING WITH THE LENDER

If a home has not already been listed for a short sale with preapproval by the lender, the process to buy will take more work on your part. While there's no guarantee the homeowner or the lender will consider a short sale, the possibility is there so it can be worth pursuing if you're interested in a particular purchase.

The steps you can expect to have to take to initiate the short sale process and get a property for less than is owed on the loan include:

• *Contacting the lender directly*

This can be a bit frustrating, but it if results in a great purchase, the work will pay off. To cut to the chase with a lender, seek out the bank that holds the deed directly when foreclosure is looming or already in process. The lending institution's name can often be found in public court records within a county. Just look up the parcel by address, or use the owner's name if you know it. Once you have the information, you will want to deal with representatives of the bank or lender's loss mitigation department directly.

- *Obtaining an authorization to release information*

This document must be signed by the homeowner to enable the lender to speak with you about the mortgage. To properly negotiate, you will need to know the details of the loan and how much the bank is still owed. Short sales cannot be considered if the property owner does not agree. While many are interested, some will hang on through foreclosure in hopes of coming up with a way to save their home.

- *Obtaining a sign off by the property owner*

The lending bank cannot sell a home out from underneath the property owner in a short sale. In order to gain the benefits of this type of purchase, the homeowner must agree to the process. During this phase, the existing homeowner will have to fill out forms, justify hardship and basically prove that they cannot pay the mortgage even if foreclosure is threatened.

• *Getting an appraisal*

Even if a lender and homeowner agree to pursue a short sale, some other work is necessary before a bottom line price will be set for the property. The lender will likely want to obtain what is called a "broker's price opinion" to gain a real understanding of a property's value. The lower the price happens to be, the more likely it is a lender will approve a short sale. You'll also very likely want to order your own appraisal, but only do so after you know the bank and homeowner are serious.

• *Making sure your financing is in order*

Unless you are funding the purchase in cash only, you will also have to satisfy the terms set forth by your lender to close a deal.

- *Obtaining the settlement statement*

Before a final sale goes through, the lending institution will want to look at such things as commissions going to real estate agents, your financing arrangement, other expenses associated with the sale and the estimated date of closing.

Once a lender agrees to a short sale and its price, the process will move like most other real estate transactions.

WORKING WITH A PREAPPROVED SHORT SALE

In today's market, it is not uncommon to come across short sales advertised as such. In these cases, the lender and homeowner have already come to an agreement and have decided to pursue this option to prevent foreclosure. The process involved in this type of short sale will be abbreviated greatly and will move forward almost like a regular sale with a few caveats to satisfy the lender. You will still have to:

- Approach the seller

- Get your own appraisal and home inspection, if desired

- Put your financing together

- Negotiate on the price if there is wiggle room included in what a bank is offering. Both the lender and the homeowner will have to agree to the price. The bank is your biggest concern, but the homeowner will want to satisfy as much of the loan as possible. Owners are often liable for the taxes owed on the difference between the outstanding loan amount and your offer. They want the gap closed as much as possible, obviously.

Preapproved short sales speed up the process and are much easier to deal with. There can be some time delays involved as lending institutions go over an offer and determine if it is in their best interest to take it.

Remember, lending companies often have shareholders to answer to, so they will go over their options with a fine-tooth comb. While it is generally more advantageous to find a pre-approved short sale deal, striking out on your own to find properties can also net some great purchase.

The truth is both scenarios, can be very beneficial when it comes to the bottom line. The reality is short sales can provide a much bigger pricing discount that even foreclosure auctions because of the timing involved in the purchase.

"Let the future tell the truth, and evaluate each one according to his work and accomplishments. The present is theirs; the future, for which I have really worked, is mine".

-. Nikola Tesla **(Scientific)**

FINDING THE PERFECT SHORT SALE OPPORTUNITY

Take a look around at houses that can be good short sale opportunities. Here are some ways that you can find those that are short sales include:

• Putting ads in the paper offering to purchase homes instead of foreclosure

• Take a look around at areas where there seems to be a lot of homes for sale

• Work with a real estate agent or get your own license

• Put signs up in the neighborhood where there are a lot of homes for sale

• Call on homes that are for sale by owner

These are a few good options when it comes to getting the short sale opportunity. Remember that you want a seller who is desperate to sell and wants to walk away from the deal without having to leave a check. More and more people are walking into closings to sell their homes with checks instead of walking away without checks. This is one of the latest trends when it comes to the buyer's market.

One thing you will want to do before you approach a potential short sale seller is to get some business cards and brochures prepared. Many people do not known what a short sale is and will naturally be skeptical when it comes to getting out of a bad deal without having to pay any money. They will think that you are out to cheat them in some manner. Most will be wary at best when it comes to accepting your offer.

If the property owner has a real estate agent they will probably be even more skeptical as their real estate agent, who they trust, will be telling them not to sell on the short sale. The reason for this is that they real estate agent will be one of the people who are going to be negotiated with when it comes to negotiating for less fees and money. And most real estate agents will want to have the entire commission for their time.

This will not always be the case when it comes to real estate agents. Some, especially those who see the house sale as being a waste of time, will be for anything that will allow them to gain some commission. The real estate agent should not be completely cut out of the picture as they can help you with some documents that you may need to complete the short sale.

When you put the ads in the paper, you will have to screen the calls to make sure that the person on the other end of the phone understands what you are offering. While you do not want to scare away a potential client, you are going to want to discover if they are a potential short sale client.

By talking to them like a friend instead of an investor, you may earn their trust and get them to tell you their financial status with regard to their property.

Remember that the owner of the property must be to the point where they need to sell right away and is probably at the point where they are thinking of ways to borrow money to get through the closing process.

After you have talked to the short sale owner on the phone you should then make an appointment to see him as soon as possible. At the meeting, the more information you know about his home, how long his home has been on the market and how many other homes are on the market in the area. What are his chances of selling this house as it stands now and what other options are there available for the seller? You are going to want to get the seller to trust you right from the start.

You can talk to owner of the property without the insurance agent present as long as you are not a licensed real estate agent yourself. It would be unethical to try to make a deal with the owner if you are an agent without the listing agent present.

Your potential seller may or may not know what a short sale is so you might have to explain to them what is going to happen during the course of the short sale and what is more important, what is in it for them.

You should have some written materials to hand him. This presentation is very important and probably one of the most crucial aspects of the deal.

The more that you understand about the process of foreclosure and the short sale, the better your presentation will be with your potential short sale seller. You should be able to explain exactly how foreclosure hurts their credit more than a bad debt write off, which is what will happen with the short sale.

You should also advise them against throwing more money into the house than they have already invested. You want to make sure that they understand how it can be a good idea to get a new start by saving that money and putting it towards a new home or opportunity. In addition to having brochures, you should also have information about your previous success when it comes to foreclosure.

Part of the foreclosure deal will be negotiating with the lenders so that they let the borrower off the hook and do not go after him with a judgment. You are going to want to make sure that the owner of the property knows that you have had a proven track record of dealing with lenders and negotiating short sale deals. You can give them references on paper of people who they can call who you have helped through the short sale process.

Remember, the more information that you have and can provide to the owner, the more professional you look and the more impressed the owner will be with your presentation. You will only get one chance to make your first impression on your potential short sale seller. Make sure that you are well dressed and look professional. Have business cards and other information in writing so that they can review it after you are gone.

Do not press them to make up their minds right away, give them time to thing about it. But then you should follow up with a phone call to see if there are any questions that they have after your presentation that they neglected to ask while you were at their home. Some people are naturally suspicious about anyone offering them a deal where they can get away with not having to pay any more of their mortgage and not have the bank foreclose on them. It is up to you to assure them that this is what you do for a living and that you are an expert in negotiations. Once the owner of the property trusts you, it is then time to get to work with the negotiation process.

ADDING UP THE NUMBERS

Okay, so you now know that short sales aren't always easy to obtain, but they can still be very worth your while. It is highly unlikely to obtain better pricing on a piece of property – even during a foreclosure auction.

Once a piece of property has gone through foreclosure, not only does a lender have the defaulted loan costs to try and recoup through a sale, but also the legal expenses attached to the foreclosure process. While foreclosures are generally bargains, they won't be "steals," per say. Lenders will be forced to squeeze every penny they can out of this type of sale. This is just not the case with short sales.

When the potential earnings off a short sale are looked at, most investors agree this is an incredible way to buy property. Even when a short sale property requires a bit of work to make it marketable, the profit margin can be quite high. Plus, it is often possible to pick up preexisting home purchases on properties that are in near pristine condition. Even fixer uppers can be well worth your while though. (We'll talk about those a little later).

To get a good idea of what a short sale purchase can mean financially, it helps to take a look at a scenario.

Let's say a payoff, and for simplicity sake the value, on a two-story home with a two-car garage is $218,000. Through short sale negotiations, you manage to buy the property at $150,000 free and clear. Now, let's say you put $5,000 into repairs and renovations to make the property more marketable to buyers. To sell the property quickly, you let it go for $200,000. This price gives the buyer instant equity, which is always attractive in a purchase situation. Plus, it would give you a profit of $45,000.

While it's true that not every short sale will have a scenario with this high of a profit margin, many do.

Banks are simply more willing to negotiate prices in a downward fashion when they haven't invested a lot of money in the legal process to foreclose.

The trick to making sure your short sale purchases are decent when it comes to profit margin involves doing your homework in advance. You need to learn how to deal with lenders directly. You also want to know the ropes of working with a real estate agent to find and purchase property that is not only worth investing in, but also likely to turn around in a fairly quick fashion.

Relying on an agent will have you paying out a commission, but it can be money well spent. This is especially so if you are unfamiliar with the communities in which you plan on buying.

Once you get the ball rolling with making short sale purchases and turning them around, you will find this method for buying can work to your advantage in a number of ways. Some of the potential perks of going with short sales include:

- Getting a purchase for the lowest possible price If you strike while the iron's hot as we mentioned before, banks will be more likely to negotiate. If you can get a property for a lot less than its value, you will be able to make a profit – even in this market and even if you have to hang on to it for a while.

- Not having to deal with foreclosure auctions While very good properties can be purchased at great prices during foreclosure auctions, this mode of buying often involves a lot of competition and it can involve an almost "blind" purchase. With short sales, you have some time to do your homework on the property, too. This is essential for helping you understand a property before you buy and what your chances for success with profits truly are.

- Helping homeowners in need Short sales not only help banks cut their losses, but they can be a real boon to homeowners who are facing financial burdens. If their obligations can be partially handled through a short sale and their records freed from a potential foreclosure, they will be better positioned to start afresh. While this might not matter to you as an investor, it can prove to be a strong altruistic motivator for some.

Purchasing a property through a short sale deal can simply give you the greatest possible profit margin to work with. In turn, this can give you the leverage you need to make your money back and then some on a resale. After all, it's always smarter to buy something for less and then turn around and sell it for more.

"A system of morality which is based on relative emotional values is a mere illusion, a thoroughly vulgar conception which has nothing sound in it and nothing true".

-. Socrates (Philosopher)

NEGOTIATING WITH SHORT SALE SELLERS

The first part of the negotiating process is with the short sale sellers. This can be easier than negotiating with the lenders, which is step two in the process. Negotiating with the sellers can be easy once they get to the point where they understand what you are doing and they can trust you. The seller owes more on the house than the house is worth. They want out of the deal. You have to get them to sign a real estate contract, or purchase and sale agreement, in which you will pay less than market value for the home and less than the seller owes. The seller, at this point, has nothing to lose by doing this. He is walking away from the closing with no money anyway.

He may balk about the price of the property being dragged down, but when push comes to shove, he is going to be happy to get out of the deal without it costing him any money. In an era where most sellers are coming to real estate closings with checks, your seller will be grateful not to have to do this. The negotiations will begin once you present the seller with the cold hard facts of his predicament. He is in a quandary. He owes more on the house than the house is worth and he is not the only person on the block who is trying to sell his house. Other sellers are also thinking of doing the same thing.

They would like to get the short sale deal just the same. Many on the block want out of the deal they are in. If your seller does not take the deal, chances are that one of his neighbors will. And that will bring the prices of the houses down anyhow. At least your seller can benefit from the process. You should show him comparables about what different houses in the area are selling for and how long they are on the market.

A real estate agent can get you this information if you do not have access to the MLS. If you are going to invest in short sales, it might behoove you to pay for access to the MLS which is the giant database where all homes listed by realtors are sold.

Access to the MLS is not restricted to realtors. Anyone can have access to the MLS for a fee. But this only tells you what is for sale in the neighborhood and how long the properties have been on the market. In order to place a value on the home, you need to find out how much money houses have been selling for in the area. This is public knowledge and can be obtained by taking a trip to county assessor's office that usually has this information. Much of this information can be also discovered online. Housing value is determined by the sale price of other houses that are similar to yours in the same area. Not the listed price, but the actual sales price.

Other factors figure in to the value once a base value has been determined. Does the house need work? Have there been any updates and if so, what kind of updates? Some updates that add to the value of the home include:

- New windows

- Maintenance free exterior (aluminum siding, fascia)

- New roof

- New driveway

- Kitchen renovation (complete updating and not just decorating)

- Bath renovation (again, not just painting but complete renovation)

- New garage

- New furnace

- Central air conditioning

- Plumbing or electrical updates

These are all structural improvements to the house and will add value. The bathroom and kitchen remodeling, if needed, will add value as long as it is not just cosmetic changes that were made. Some things that make the house easier to sell but do not add value are:

• Finishing a basement

• Installing new carpet or tile

• Getting new appliances

• Exterior or interior painting

• New interior doors or woodwork

• Minor room renovations

Again, the above list are some things that people will notice right 18 away and are relatively cheap to accomplish. If you are seeking a way to sell a house in a hurry, get rid of the old carpet and paint everything.

Make some minor cosmetic changes (such as a change of old fashioned light fixtures) and you can have a better chance of selling the house. But cosmetic changes do not add value when the house is being appraised. This is what you will have to make note of before you begin negotiating with your short sale seller.

Before you meet with the seller, you should have as much information as possible so that you can give them an honest approximate value of their home. The seller may have no idea how much their home is worth.

Chances are that they see other homes in the area that are for sale and have even called on some of them. If they have chosen a real estate agent, the agent should have shown them comparables. This would be a few houses like their home and the sale price of these homes. This would give them an idea of the value.

The agent also should have measured the rooms and also taken note of anything that could have added to the value of the home. Although they are not real estate appraisers, real estate agents are trained in determining home valuation so that they can accurately price the home. When you sit down and talk to the seller, you should have a pretty good idea of the valuation of the home in question.

You should have a good idea of other homes in the area that have been for sale and how long they have been on the market. You will then have to observe what needs work in your seller's home. You are better off to present your proposal in writing to the seller. You do not have to present them with a real estate contract right off the bat, but this is a good way of letting him or her know that you are serious.

Prior to presenting them with the contract, you want to sit down and talk to them about how you came up with the price. You also need to know how much the seller is behind on their mortgage, if any amount, and how much is owed. One other bit of due diligence you should complete before you actually sit down with the seller and offer them money for their property is a quick title search.

You can order what is known as an O & E, which stands for Owner and Encumbrances. This is not a formal title search and you are going to still need to do a formal search before you actually purchase the property.

The O&E will let you know who owns the property and what type of encumbrances are on the property. Any mortgage is recorded against the property as well as any liens. Again, the more you know about the property before going in, the better off you will be.

Here is a checklist of items you will want to determine before making a proposal to the owner of the property for the short sale:

• Is the owner of the property the person with whom you are negotiating?

• How much is the property worth?

• How many other homes are on the market in the area and for how long?

• What type of updates are in the property and what type of improvements are needed?

• How much is owed on the property?

• Is there more than one mortgage?

- Are the taxes paid?

- Are there any liens on the property, such as mechanic's liens?

You do not need a title search to discover this information. A trip to the county building where the property is located will tell you everything you need to know about the property. Any liens or encumbrances against the property have to be recorded. Anything recorded against a piece of property is pubic knowledge.

You can determine this information in the county recorder's office. In some cases, the information is on computer, in others, you have to look it up by hand. Each time the property is conveyed to a new owner, a deed is recorded.

All previous mortgages should be paid off at that time. When a mortgage is paid off, a release is recorded.

The only thing that a title company does is pulls up information that is public record. When a mortgage is recorded against the property, the amount of the mortgage will be public knowledge.

Although you will not know if the seller has defaulted on that as it will not be recorded. If the recorded mortgage is for $130,000, and the seller has not paid the mortgage in a few months, the amount might have risen. You can get a rough idea of how much is owed by when the mortgage has been recorded.

A mortgage holder pays off mostly interest and very little premium during the first few years of the loan. The older the loan gets, the more principal gets paid off and the less interest. Towards the end of the loan, the borrower is paying more principal and very little interest.

The name of the party to whom the deed is conveyed is also listed on the deed. You want to make sure that you are dealing with the owner of the property and that the owner is not in a nursing home and a nephew or relative is not trying to sell the house from under them.

Taxes can be a problem. They have to be paid up or the county can actually take the property. They will have more jurisdiction than the bank and unlike a mortgage loan, taxes cannot be negotiated.

The information on how much the taxes are and if they are paid can be ascertained at the county assessor's office. Once you have done all of the research into the property, you are ready to negotiate with the owner of the property. You are going to want to point out all of the reasons why it will benefit them to sell the house to you and get out now.

The multitude of homes on the market that are not selling. The amount of money that they owe that will continue to escalate. The fact that it is unlikely that they will get their price (show them what other homes are selling for), the defects in the house (if any), and the fact that the longer they stay in the property, the more taxes can be assessed. You will also want to tell them a little bit about a foreclosure.

If the lender forecloses upon them, they will not only take the house, but if they owe more than the value of the house, they can just as easily get a judgment against the borrower for any other amount due, including attorney's fees, which can be quite substantial.

You do not want to offend the seller, but you do want to give him a hard does of reality. If he owes more than the house is worth, is it really wise to continue to keep living there and paying a mortgage and taxes on this bad investment? And if he sells it, does he really want to throw good money after bad and bring a check to the closing when he can save that money towards a new house? The argument that you will have to overcome from the owner is that they do not want any bad marks on their credit.

Some people are willing to pay thousands of dollars to maintain a credit score, which is something that has become a source of concern over the past 10 years.

Credit scores are simply a marketing device that are used in a variety of different ways to get you to borrow more money than you need. If the seller is in over his head, perhaps it is time he stopped borrowing to live and started living within his means.

Another myth about credit scores is that those with a low credit score will not be able to borrow money. Not true. You can be bankrupt and still get a home loan. You just have to go to secondary market. If your seller is behind on his mortgage, his credit score is already suffering.

However, he can refrain from having a foreclosure on his credit history by going through with the short sale. The lender, after negotiations, will write the loan off as a bad debt.

This will go on his credit but will not look as bad as a foreclosure. He will still be able to obtain credit and after a certain number of years, the event will be entirely erased from his credit history. It is far wiser for anyone never to throw good money after bad. If a seller has a poor investment in a home, it is better for them to get out and save any cash that they have for the future so that they can rebuild.

Not give it to the bank so that they can maintain a marketing tool such as a "credit score."

Typical Negotiation:

In a typical short sale negotiation with the seller, the short sale investor has done his or her homework and knows everything they need to know about the house.

They know the following:

• John Smith is the owner

• There are 32 other properties in the immediate vicinity for sale, 24 the average time span for the properties on the market is 9 months

• The property is worth $120,000, although it was purchased at $150,000 and is listed at $135,000

• Mr. Smith owes $130,000 on the property

• The taxes are current and there are no liens on the property

• The original mortgage was paid off and refinanced - it looks as if Mr. Smith took out equity

• The house needs a new roof and the bathroom needs updating. All of the above information can be obtained prior to your meeting with Mr. Smith.

You have it all printed out on paper. Mr. Smith owes the bank $130,000. He took out the loan two years ago which means that he probably only paid about $1,000, if that, against the principal. He is not current in his mortgage. You go over all of the above with Mr. Smith, excluding the fact that he is the owner and that you checked up on him.

You then bring up the fact that there are 32 other properties selling that are in better condition than his: his property needs a new roof and the bathroom needs to be updated. You bring up what he can expect with a foreclosure. How it can hurt his credit. Then you tell him how you can help.

You can negotiate with the mortgage company to let him walk away from his $130,000 debt without having to pay any more money. 25 The offer that you make to Mr. Smith is $105,000 for his house. This is $15,000 less than the property is worth in its current condition and $25,000 less than he owes the bank. He will protest that this is less than what he wants, but with your deal, he gets to walk away from the sale without bringing a check to the closing, without having to pay any more mortgage payments.

He can save the money he was willing to pay towards the closing towards another house, which he will be able to get even with the hit against his credit with the bad debt. You then explain to him again the unlikelihood of him selling his house at $130,000.

You tell him that you can even take care of the amount he will have to pay in commission to the real estate agent. Then you give him your signed purchase and sale agreement for $105,000 and tell him to think it over. This is a typical negotiation.

The seller might be upset because he is not getting the price for his property, but he is getting a better deal - a way out that is not going to cost him a bit of money. And as he is struggling to pay his mortgage on a property that is worth less than what he owes, he will most likely take the deal. After the seller agrees to the short sale, you have to kick into gear and prepare the documents so that you can make the deal with the lender.

"I do not know what I may appear to the world, but to myself I seem to have been only like a boy playing on the seashore, and diverting myself in now and then finding a smoother pebble or a prettier shell than ordinary, whilst the great ocean of truth lay all undiscovered before me".

-. Isaac Newton (Scientific)

THE SHORT SALE DOCUMENT PACKAGE

Once the seller agrees to the short sale proposal, you have to then put together a package to give to the lender so that they will also agree to the concept. Although you will be offering the lender less money than is owed on the property, they will be inclined to accept a reasonable offer. They know that the foreclosure process takes a long time and is expensive.

They also know that once the house is foreclosed upon and goes back to the lender, they have to sell it, usually at a loss. Many times, it is a mess by the time the foreclosure is finalized, which can take up to a year.

Yes, they can get a judgment against the borrower for attorney's fees and any amount due, but try to collect on that judgment. If the seller is out of work and has no assets, or better yet, declares bankruptcy, they are out of luck. And this judgment is one of the few that can be dismissed in a bankruptcy court. So the lender has an incentive to go along with the short sale because in the long run, it will end up saving them money.

Negotiating with the lender is usually easier than the seller, who doesn't understand the concept. The lender is fully aware of what you are trying to do but will still try to squeeze extra money from you. The first thing you need to do when the seller accepts your offer is call the lender and find out who is responsible for the short sales.

You will probably get bounced around from department to department. You might get a better deal at a larger lending institution which is more prepared for the write off, but you will have to wait longer for an answer and may have to deal with several different people.

Once you discover who the person is to whom you have to submit information, talk to them, touch base, tell them what you are doing and that you are planning on purchasing a property on which they hold the mortgage that is in default or will soon be going into default. Tell them that you are sending them a package of information and ask them if there is anything else they need.

The documents that you will need to send to facilitate the short sale with the mortgage company are as follows:

• Purchase and Sale Agreement

• Consent Form

• Hardship Letter

• Comparables of other real estate sales

• Your financing information

• Seller financing information (possibly)

Purchase and Sale Agreement

The purchase and sale agreement, or real estate contract, will not have any contingencies except for one - that is clear title. You want to make sure that you get a house that is free and clear of any encumbrances. This means that in order for the deal to go through, the lender has to issue a release of the mortgage.

There can be no financial contingencies on the real estate contract. No inspection contingencies. All of your due diligence regarding the state of the home should be done prior to submitting the proposal to the lender. The only thing you should be concerned with is getting clear title. If the lender has been paying the taxes from escrow, you are going to want to make sure that all taxes continue to be paid up to date.

You may be liable for some back taxes if the seller is behind on their mortgage payments, but if they are only a couple of months behind, there should still be money in escrow to keep the taxes current. If the seller has been paying their own taxes, this is part of your own due diligence and not the problem of the lender.

Be advised that all taxes will have to be paid to date in order for you to get clear title. The purchase and sale agreement will list the fact that you are ready to close and how much you are willing to pay for the house. Any financing contingencies can be crossed out. There should be no attorney review rider - if you want your attorney to review the purchase and sale agreement, do so prior to submitting it to the bank. You have to be willing, able and ready to close the property in 30 days.

Consent Form

The consent form is a letter from the borrower to the lender authorizing them to discuss their mortgage with you. As you are a third party, the lender will not discuss the state of the mortgage with you without written consent from the borrower. This document should be dated and notarized and signed by all parties on the mortgage. It should list your name and the mortgage loan number.

Hardship Letter

This is something that should actually come from the seller but is a document that you can help him prepare. This is a letter that states why the borrower can no longer fulfill their obligation to make payments on their mortgage.

The worse off the borrower appears, the better off for the deal. If the reason for the default is one of the following, you have a better chance of having the short sale approved by the lender:

- Loss of job
- Illness
- Divorce
- Death in the family

In addition to stating why the borrower can no longer afford his obligation, the letter should also give testament to his sorry state of financial affairs. The fact that he has no money, no prospects and is suffering from emotional distress because of the situation.

Remember that you want clear title. The lender has to be convinced that they are not going to be able to squeeze any more money out of their borrower and that it will be better off to write off the bad debt.

They cannot put the borrower into prison because he cannot pay his mortgage - there are no more debtor's prisons in society. The only thing they can do is get a judgment on them and then try to enforce the judgment. This can be impossible if the borrower has no money or job. And again, if the borrower files bankruptcy, the mortgage company gets nothing.

You can write the hardship letter for the seller and go over it with him and then have him sign the letter. The letter must be signed by the seller/borrower.

Comparables of other real estate sales

The more information you can give to state your case to the lender as to why they should take a loss and accept your offer the better. If there are 32 houses on the market that are all sitting there, unsold, chances are that if the lender grabs the house in a foreclosure, there are going to be 33. If the houses are not selling and the market in the area is dead, it is in the best interest of the lender to take the deal.

You can get comparables at the county assessor's office or even online. Remember that these are sale prices of homes in the area that are like the home in question and not listed prices. In addition to the value of the home by comparables, you should also list (if true) the number of homes that are in the area that are for sale.

This gives the lender an incentive to want to take the deal. This information should be formatted to build a case in your favor. In the area cited in the previous chapter, the lender is taking a loss of $25,000.

There has to be an incentive for them to do this. If they feel that even if taking over the property they are unlikely to sell it for the market value and that they are going to take a bigger loss if they go through with foreclosure (not to mention that the foreclosure will take a while at which time the house is liable to be in worse condition than it is now) they will take the deal. The lender will weight the checks and balances. You have to offer them a better deal than a foreclosure.

Your financial information

In order to make the short sale fly with the lender, you are going to have to show proof that you are able to close on the property in 30 days. This proof entails either bank statements that reflect enough cash in the account or a pre-approval letter from a mortgage company. The lender is not concerned with how you finance the property as long as there are not contingencies.

Again, you do not have to purchase a short sale with cash. You can finance the deal but your financing has to be pre-approved. This means that you have to get a pre-approval letter from the bank. A pre-approval letter is not a pre-qualification letter. A pre-approval letter is a letter from the underwriter that states that you are approved for a mortgage up to a certain amount.

They have reviewed the purchase and sale agreement and the only contingency is clear title (which is on the purchase and sale agreement anyway).

They are ready to give you the money as you have submitted all supporting documents (proof of employment, income tax statements, financial information) to the lender. The lender is ready to close on the property.

Usually, a lender will only loan you 80 percent of the amount of the sale price. So you should also present the short sale lender with proof of your down payment. This should be a bank statement reflecting the amount of the down payment in your bank account. One word about submitting bank account statements.

You should submit three months worth of statements to the lender. Lenders are under an obligation not to deal with people who suddenly deposit large sums of cash into their bank account. They will want to know where this cash came from.

It is better if you have bank statements that reflect a solid balance for more than one month. If you are using investors, you should submit the information of a joint venture and a bank statement from the venture to the lender. We will discuss alternate financing for a short sale investment in the next chapter.

Seller's financial information

Remember, if the seller is in dire straits, the better off for your deal. The lender knows they cannot squeeze blood out of a stone so if you submit banking information and statements from your seller stating that he only has $300 to his name, the lender will be more inclined to take the deal, although the lender will run a credit check on the borrower, so this information should be true. The seller's financial information does not necessarily have to be part of the short sale package.

"There is a huge need and a huge opportunity to get everyone in the world connected, to give everyone a voice and to help transform society for the future. The scale of the technology and infrastructure that must be built is unprecedented, and we believe this is the most important problem we can focus on".

-. Mark Zuckerberg (Facebook)

SHORT SALE INVESTORS

The more you understand about the short sale, the better off you will be. You can use your knowledge to convince investors to go along with you in the deal. Some investors will be willing to enter into a joint venture with you so that they can make easy money with little financial risk to themselves and not much effort. If you have the know-how when it comes to short sales, you can find someone with cash or borrowing power and form a joint venture.

A joint venture is like a partnership that is limited to a particular project. In this case, the project would be the short sale investment. You can have an attorney draw up documents that reflect everyone's responsibility with regards to the project. The responsibility of the financial backer will be to finance the project once the short sale is complete and the closing is set.

The beauty of this type of investment that you want to stress to any investor is that no money actually has to change hands until the day of the real estate closing. Unlike buying a foreclosure, you do not have to put down a cash deposit on the property - just prove that you have the cash to close.

The only risk for the investor is if the house turns out to be worth even less than you pay for it. This is why it will be so important for you to do due diligence prior to the sale. You are going to have to show all of this information to the investor.

We will discuss due diligence and title issues a following chapter. For the most part, the investor just has to put up the money for the closing and then wait for the property to be sold at which time he gets half of the profit.

Depending on what kind of deal you make, the return can be exceptional. It will be much more than the investor can get for a bank investment and much less risky than a stock investment. The ideal short sale investor is someone who understands a bit about the real estate market but does not have the time or the inclination to negotiate the deal with the bank and the seller.

This person can be an attorney, doctor or anyone who wants to make a good return on a real estate investment that can occur only in a down market. You can divide the proceeds of the sale of the investment in any way you like. You may have more than one investor in the joint venture.

If you are planning on investing in the property as a joint venture, you are going to have to have legal documents drawn up by an attorney and will have to present them to the lender as well as the closing agent so that the joint venture can take title to the property.

In some states, a joint venture cannot take title. If this is the case in your state, you can simply have everyone who is involved in the joint venture take title as tenants in common.

This means that everyone will get a share of the proceeds of the property. If one of the partners dies, their share will go to their estate and not to the other partners.

You can find short sale investors by joining investor clubs or talking to people who are interested in making an investment. Some people have found that pooling their money together makes for good short sale investments.

Start an investment club either online or locally for those who are interested in taking advantage of the buyer's market that we are now experiencing in the real estate industry. This can be a good way to meet others who would like to also invest in this type of real estate venture.

How to find potential buys

Now that you have a better idea of what's involved with the short sale process and how much money can actually be made, it's time to start looking for some properties to consider buying.

There are several options on this front. One involves going it alone completely. The other two options will require that you work with real estate agents.

All three can net you some very good purchases. You'll likely save yourself some money by going it alone, but working with an agent can help you find buys that are potentially better and more marketable when you're ready to put an exit plan into action.

Going it alone

This can be a very time consuming process and it will require that you have a lot of patience. If a short sale hasn't already been discussed between a homeowner and a lender, there are no guarantees that this is an option.

The homeowner might have reasons to want to hang on to a property. The bank might not be short sale friendly. You will have to spend time pursuing to find out for certain. Still, it is possible that by initiating the process and suggesting the idea personally, you could land yourself a very good deal without competition involved.

To find properties that might be good candidates for short sales, you'll want to look for homes that are listed as "lis pendens" in the court system. This indicates that the lender has begun the foreclosure process by notifying the homeowner of its intend to do so.

While the foreclosure process has technically started at this point, you might be able to entice both the homeowner and lender into accepting an offer that's reasonable.

If you are successful, the homeowner will escape foreclosure and the bank will save itself time and money on taking the foreclosure process through to fruition.

To find properties in the lis pendens stage of foreclosure, you'll want to scour your local court system for filings. In many jurisdictions you can do this using the Internet.

In some cases, the search engine on the court system's Web site will let you sort listings by action type, which means you can readily locate lis pendens filings.

If you do find a property you're interested in, you'll want to contact the lender that filed the paperwork in court. Speaking with the homeowner directly is also not a bad idea.

Should both the lender and homeowner agree to consider a short sale, you'll go through the process as described previously. As you wait for answers, you can do some preliminary research on the property to see if it's a good candidate for purchase or not.

It is also possible to look for pre-approved short sales on your own. This will prevent you from having to hire an agent to help, but you might have to deal with the seller's representative.

To go this route, you'll want to look in the usual places for real estate listings that are short sales, or listed as preforeclosure. The places to look include:

• Newspaper classifieds

- Real estate Web sites
- Local MLS systems, if you have access
- Real estate fliers and other advertising vehicles.

HOW AGENTS CAN HELP YOU

If you'd rather fast-track the process of finding short sale properties, working with a real estate agent is the best way to go. Your options here include:

- **Hiring your own agent**

You can enlist a real estate agent to help you find potential short sale buys. While some might not want to do this, many are willing especially when the market is down and sales are sluggish.

Agents will know how to use the local MLS system to find properties that are negotiable in a short sale. The truth of the matter is that not all short sales are listed as such. Code phrases like "subject to bank approval," "auction bound" and even "subject to bank approval" can all be tip offs. Agents will know what to look for, but you might not.

- **Looking at listings and working with a seller's agent**

When a home has been set for a short sale the homeowner or the lender might hire an agent to list and represent the property. If you are interested in a specific property and know it's a short sale, this can be the fastest way to go to find out more about the property and whether it's worth pursuing or not.

Short sales are not in short supply at the moment. Whether you go it alone or enlist the help of a real estate professional, you are likely to come across very good buys. Keep in mind that a lender will do its best to get you to pay the highest amount and so will an agent that represents a lender. It's your job – or your agent's – to help you strike a deal that works to your advantage, as well.

"In business, you invest when things are not in good shape. When you invest at these times, you take a better position than your competitors. When there is a recession and your competition does not invest, they are giving you the advantage".

-. **Carlos Slim (Businessman)**

LENDER NEGOTIATIONS

After you present the package of information to the lender regarding the short sale that contains all the pertinent documents, you are then going to have to follow up with the lender. Chances are that they are going to take a while to give you an answer with regard to the deal. The average time span between the time you submit the package to the lender and when you get an answer is 60 days. Lenders are inundated with requests for short sales. Each request must be carefully reviewed by the lender and the checks and balances weighed.

The lender is fully aware of the options and wants to make the deal that will cost them the least amount of money, If you are a good investor and are offering cash, you will get preference over someone who is offering to buy the property with a mortgage. Even with a pre-approval letter, a lender would rather deal with a cash sale. However, this should not put you off from trying the short sale with financing. The lender has three options with regard to your proposal of the short sale.

These are the options:

- No Deal

- Yes, Lets Close

- Yes, at a higher price

These are the options. Many times, the lender will choose option number three which is basically a counter offer for the purchase of the property. In the scenario described earlier in this book, we looked at a very reasonable and conservative offer with regard to the short sale. The property was worth $420.000,00; the owner owed $430.000,00 and we offered $350.000,00. The lender may come back and ask for $390.000,00. Whether or not you choose to take the deal depends on several different factors.

Are you planning on selling this house or are you planning on living in this house?

Are you looking at this property as a short term investment or a long term investment?

Are you sharing the proceeds with anyone?

If you are seeking to purchase the property as a primary residence, this can be a good deal for you. You are getting the property at less than market value. If you feel that this is a place where you wish to live and that the prices of the homes dropped due to an influx of homes for sale in the market, they are very likely to rebound once the real estate market picks up. If you are seeking to rent the property out, you may think about taking the deal as well if you have renters who will cover the mortgage and taxes.

Remember, you are still getting the property for less than market value. If you are planning on selling the property, this can be a toss-up. The market value of the property is $420.000,00 and you are buying it for $350.000,00. Don't forget that you are going to have to pay for any property sales taxes and title charges as this is part of the deal with the owner of the property.

Now your profit, if you sell it yourself, is about $70.000,00. If you can get market value. How many homes are on the market and will you be able to flip it? If you make some cosmetic repairs to the home and fix the roof, you may be able to raise the value to $430.000,00 so you may be able to earn a bit more in profit.

Figure on what your time is worth in the project and how much you will be expected to put forth to sell the property. The more you can do to cosmetically enhance the property yourself, the better off you are. Even if you make a few thousand dollars on a short sale all for yourself, it is not a bad investment if you are doing this on the side. A few thousand dollars for tying up your money for a month or so is not a bad return and is a lot better than you can expect to get anywhere else. If you have to split the proceeds with others, however, you may feel that the deal is not worth further negotiations. You may choose to walk away from the deal. At this point, you lose nothing.

The seller cannot force you to adhere to the purchase and sale agreement because he cannot give you clear title. The lender is not willing to release the mortgage for less than $400.000,00. You can call the lender and try to negotiate somewhere in the middle, say $390.000,00.

You can also ask that the seller pick up some of the costs outside of closing to make the deal go through. Some of the costs that he seller can take on are the title charges which are traditionally a seller's burden anyway and the county and state sales taxes. If you feel the property is worth fighting for, you need to negotiate with the lender for a better deal.

In most cases, the lender will not want to lose a good deal over a few thousand dollars. And since the seller is now way behind in the mortgage, he or she will want the deal to go through as well.

Negotiating with the lender is only difficult because the person to whom you are speaking has to get an answer from someone else, usually a committee of people. In most cases, however, the lender is more than willing to negotiate if they come back with a counter offer. If the lender comes back with a counter offer that is in the ballpark for you, you are wise to counter the counter offer and squeeze a few thousand dollars extra out of them. Remember that every dollar counts.

WORKING WITH LENDERS

Dealing with lenders in a short sale situation does require a special touch. Even though many lenders are motivated to agree to short sales at this time, it doesn't mean they are happy about it. There are a few things you need to know about to be able to properly negotiate with a lender.

Short sales are generally only agreed to by lenders when a homeowner has no equity in a home either because the loan wasn't paid down enough for this or the value of the property has dropped. Also, the homeowner must demonstrate that ability to pay the mortgage is no longer there for whatever reason. The homeowner must also prove that he or she is unable to pay the difference between your offered price and the full amount of the loan.

If you initiate the short sale process and lenders and homeowners agree to it, the homeowner will have to prove financial hardship. This is usually handled in the form of a hardship letter, which is sort of like a loan application in reverse. The difference is the seller will be trying to prove inability to pay rather than creditworthiness.

TIPS FOR HANDLING OFFERS

Once you start the negotiation process on a property, you'll want to keep these things in mind when dealing with the homeowner and the selling lender:

- **Never offer the seller money directly unless it's in the form of an offer to the bank or lender**

While the seller will have to approve of your offer, no money can go into his or her hands. Sellers will sometimes ask for kickbacks. This is illegal.

Remember, the lender is selling the property for less than is owed. The seller is expected to walk away with nothing.

- **Submit offer documentation to the lender**

Even if the seller agrees to your offer, you will have to get the lender's approval, too. You won't have a sale until the lender agrees. Make sure the lender sees your offer and receives all documentation it requests.

- **Consider offering a deposit**

This can motivate a lender to accept and offer and move faster with the process. If the lending bank knows the offer is genuine, it can work in your favor.

- **Make certain your offer is contingent on a deadline**

Even if they a motivated to sell and accept your offer, lenders can drag their feet on finalizing the closing process with short sales. This is simply because of the bureaucracy involved in many banking institutions. To protect yourself and your time, make sure you place a deadline on your offer. Do make sure your offer goes to the correct person at the lending institution and set a deadline for at least a few weeks out to be fair.

- **Do retain the right to inspect the property**

Before you close a deal, you will want to have the property appraised and fully inspected. In many cases, short sales will require some work to bring them up to a marketable condition. You need to know exactly what you are getting into if you want to make the most out of your investment.

- **Be prepared for the potential of having to pay real estate commissions**

While the lender will likely pay some, if you hire an agent directly, you might have to kick in a bit. Lenders will try to negotiate commission fees down as much as they can to recover as much of their loan as possible. The fees they pay will then be split between the lender's agent and yours, if you have one.

Working with lenders isn't as difficult as it might sound. It just requires a firm touch and some patience.

"A pessimist sees the difficulty in every opportunity; an optimist sees the opportunity in every difficulty".

-. Wiston Churchill (Ex-Minister UK)

REAL ESTATE AGENTS NEGOTIATIONS

How to handle the relationship between yourself and real estate agents when working on short sales will hinge on whether the agent works for you or the lender. The more prepared you are for both situations, the more likely it is you will get what you want out of either relationship.

Working with Real estate agents

Hiring your own agent

While it is not always necessary to hire an agent to help you locate short sale properties and close deals, it can be very useful. When an agent works on your side, you can gain benefit from their experience, their local knowledge and their ability to help you obtain the best deal possible.

Of course, you might have to pay for the service. Some agents, however, will be willing to take the split the lender offers upon closing.

Hiring an agent to assist in short sale purchases is much like finding an agent for any other real estate transaction. To get the best, it is smart to look for those who:

• **Specialize or are experienced with short sales**

Face it; short sales are not the typical kind of purchase. When an agent is experienced in closing deals like this, you will be better positioned for dealing with homeowners and lenders. Your agent's level of expertise can be a big asset during the short sale process.

- **Have a good deal of local knowledge**

This is essential to assist you in selecting the best possible buys. While a short sale price might seem fair to you, an agent will know if there are mitigating circumstances that could make the property worth less on the resale than it might seem.

For example, impending construction projects in a neighborhood could impact value. Unless you have a lot of area knowledge, it's not a bad idea to rely on an agent who knows the community you're interested in.

- **Fit with your personality**

Even if a Realtor has the best reputation in the world, if he or she doesn't fit your personality, you're not going to be happy with the situation. You want an agent you can communicate with and trust in.

It might not be necessary to hire an agent to help you find short sales, but it can work to your advantage.

The lender will likely have a broker or agent working on its side and will have access to legal help, as well.

Just remember, you might end up having to pay a portion of the commission yourself. If the agent helps you get your hands on a great buy, however, it will be worth every penny.

Working With A Lender's Agent

Should you decide to forego your own representation, it's okay. You will very likely have to deal with a seller or lender's agent, however.

There are some things you need to keep in mind when doing this. Remember, the seller's agent will:

• Not be working in your best interests, per say. He or she will represent the seller or the bank, not you.

• Will try to push you for the highest offer possible. This only makes sense considering his or her commission could depend on it.

No, you don't have to be suspicious of every move a seller's agent makes. Just keep in mind that this person wants to close the deal and get the best price possible for the clients. That's the job they were hired for, after all.

"Happiness is the secret ingredient for successful businesses. If you have a happy company it will be invincible".

-. **Richard Branson (Virgin)**

DUE DILIGENCE

Let's say that you got the deal and you are ready to close. The next step is to get a title commitment ordered. This is usually the responsibility of the seller and the seller is probably most likely using an attorney. The attorney will want to get the title ordered at a company where he can get money for examining the title. If the seller is paying for the Owner's Policy, which is what you will be getting, then traditionally they will choose the title company.

If, however, you have made a deal that you will pay for title, you should make sure that the purchase and sale agreement stipulates that the title company will be that of your choosing. You can still opt for the seller's attorney's choice, but make sure that you shop around and they give you a good deal.

The seller's attorney gets money for examining the title, which is his incentive for wanting to use a certain title company. This is not illegal. But you should not have to pay extra to feed your seller's attorney. Make sure the rate that you are paying for title is competitive. It is usually based upon the sales price of the home. As far as house inspections, you have to do this prior to the deal.

Remember, there are no contingencies allowed on the purchase and sale agreement. Prior to buying the house, you can choose to do a home inspection. You can eliminate this need if the owner is a new owner and had a home inspection, if the municipality where the home is being sold requires a municipal home inspection or if the property is new construction.

Otherwise, you should get the inspection finished before you send the package to the lender and negotiate the purchase agreement with the seller. You are entitled to get a copy of the title commitment that will be sent to the seller's attorney. Again, the only stipulation on that purchase and sale agreement should be clear title.

The seller is obligated to give you free and clear title. If you did your homework, you should have an idea of any liens that are on the property and have them worked out prior to the closing.

You are going to want a warranty deed from the seller warranting that he or she has not done anything to the property to interfere with the enjoyment of the property. You are going to want an Owner's Title Policy from the title company in the amount of the sale price of the home. Do not let anyone talk you out of getting either of these documents.

The seller should warrant the property and the title company should stick by their search and insure their findings. Here are some things that can go wrong when you purchase a house for cash and you do not get a warranty deed or title insurance policy:

• The seller can take out a second mortgage a few days after the title insurance commitment was issued and it will not reflect on the commitment. But the lien will be placed on the property. If the seller skips out without issuing a warranty deed and you do not have an owner's policy, you are stuck with the lien on the property

• The title company can make a mistake and might miss a mechanic's lien on the property

• The seller can not be the legal owner of the property

• The seller could have sold the house to someone else a few days before your sale which would not be picked up on the title search.

There are a lot of things that can happen between the time the title company does the title search and the deal closes. This is why you want an Owner's Policy.

The owner's policy will require the seller sign an ALTA statement that states he has not encumbered the property. The title company will or should do a gap search. If anything like the above goes wrong and the seller is crooked or the title company makes a mistake, you have not one but two ways to seek retribution.

You can go after the seller (he warranted that there was nothing to interfere with the enjoyment of the property) and you can go after the title company (you will make a claim against the company).

If you are not familiar with reading a title commitment or know the difference between a title insurance policy and a commitment, you should seek the assistance of a real estate attorney to review the closing documents for you.

You will also want to make sure that the property you are buying is indeed, the house in question. This is also ascertained by the title insurance commitment and policy. You should have a survey ordered that includes a site plan of how the property sits on the lot.

The survey should include a metes and bounds description which should match the metes and bounds description on the title commitment as well as that on the deed. This is also known as the legal description of the property. This is how the property is described on the county maps.

The street address of the property (123 Main Street) is merely the "commonly known as address". The real address is the metes and bounds description (beginning at the Northwesterly corner of Main and running easterly 30 degrees, 4 minutes, 3 seconds…) Some legal descriptions can be very lengthy, so it makes sense to have a shorter, common address to get your mail.

Also included in the deed and the title commitment is the tax identification number. This is assigned by the county assessor. It should be the same on the deed as well as on the title policy. It is not always reflected on the survey.

The documents and items that you should receive from the seller at the closing are:

- An Affidavit of Title
- Bill of Sale
- Seller's Closing Statement
- HUD-1 Closing Statement
- Title Insurance Policy
- Keys to the house

The deed will be sent to your in the mail after it has been recorded. Until you get the deed, the affidavit of title is your evidence of the conveyance. The Bill of Sale covers any items in the house that were sold that were not part of the house (garage door openers, window treatments, appliances, ceiling fans).

The Seller should prepare a closing statement (his attorney will do this) and the HUD-1 is the closing statement that will be prepared by the title company.

The title insurance policy may be issued right at the closing. You want to make sure that it is good from the day of closing. Of course, you want to collect keys and garage door openers at the closing as well, unless you are giving the parties extra time to move out.

Note: *If you are giving the owner of the property some time to move out, get a title indemnity from the title insurance company. This means that they have to put forth some money that will be returned to them once they move out and the house is found to be in good condition.*

Once you have successfully closed the short sale, it is then up to you do decide what you want to do with the house.

"I am convinced that most people can achieve their dreams and beyond if they have the determination to keep trying."

-. **Howard Schultz (Starbucks)**

MAKING SURE THE PRICE IS RIGHT

Dealing with offers and counteroffers in a short sale situation can be a little tricky. It's your job to settle on the lowest possible price. It's the seller's and the bank's, of course, to get the most money possible.

As the back and forth goes back and forth, there are some things you'll want to do to make sure even a low price is a fair price.

Considering the fluctuations in the market as of late, you will want an appraisal. You'll also likely want to obtain a home inspection and a detailed list of work that might need to be done to make the house marketable at a much higher price.

With this in mind, preliminary contractor estimates are also in order so you can have a much better understanding of your true costs.

WHY YOU NEED AN APPRAISAL

The whole point of buying a short sale property is to gain as much instant equity in a purchase as possible. The greater this number happens to be, the more your final profit will be in all likelihood. While your offer will be for less than what the homeowner owes on a loan, you also want it to be less than the true value of the home.

The only way to know exactly what you're getting into with a purchase as far as value is concerned is to order an appraisal. You can bet the lender will do the same. Make sure an appraisal is thorough and includes comparisons with other recently sold properties in the area. Property value drops are not common, but recent history has produced some rather large ones. Knowing where you stand before you make a final offer is essential.

Remember, if you're going through a lender to finance your purchase, an appraisal will be needed anyway.

When you get an appraisal, along with an inspection and estimates of repair costs, you'll be better positioned to:

• Make a reasonable offer that will provide you with a profit margin

• Obtain your own financing

• Determine how much to spend on repairs that might be necessary

• Arrive at a fair selling price when you're ready to put the purchase back on the market.

Trying to buy a short sale without an appraisal is just not smart. This extra expense is a small one in the grand scheme of things and it can help you avoid a very bad purchase.

THE IMPORTANCE OF HOME INSPECTIONS

To make sure you're putting your money into a sound purchase, you will want to reserve and exercise the right to have a home inspection performed. Don't rely on the seller or lender's home inspection report. While home inspectors are generally very honest, it's just best to have one working on your side, at your expense.

Getting a home inspection can help you with such things as:

• **Obtaining your own financing**

Some lenders will require that you have an inspection performed so they can make sure their investment in a piece of property is sound.

• **Creating an offer**

If a lot of repairs are necessary, you will want to know it to help you formulate a decent offer. The cost of these repairs can be deducted from your offer price and they may impact the current valuation on a property. When you have a full inspection report, you can show a seller and lender exactly why you've come in with a low ball offer on a short sale that already involves a low ball price.

• **Estimating your costs for resale**

A home inspector will go over the entire property with a fine-tooth comb. This is essential for helping you determine your potential financial exposure in preparing a purchase for resale. You need to know about major flaws in the home and minor ones, too.

• **Determining if a purchase is worth it**

If a home inspector comes back with a report that a property is seriously flawed, it might behoove you to walk away. If the problems are structural or hidden from view in the walls or attic spaces, the only way you're going to find out about them is to have an inspector take a look at the property. Just think about it. Buying a $100,000 house for $50,000 won't seem like a steal if you have to pay $45,000 to fix structural problems, termite damage, plumbing issues and even footing the bill for electrical system repairs can take a big bite out of potential profits.

While it is more than possible to purchase a property without ordering your own inspection, it's just not wise. If you buy without knowing what you're getting into, you could discover that your excellent buy has turned into a money pit.

OBTAINING PRELIMINARY QUOTES FROM CONTRACTORS

Once you have an inspection report in hand, it's a good idea to start estimating your costs for repairs. While contractors won't be able to give you completely accurate estimates until they can get into the property, you can start getting preliminary cost figures from them.

This will help you determine if the price of the purchase combined with the estimated costs of repairs is worth the potential profit margin that will result. Contractors can also give you an idea of how long you'll have to wait to get the work done so you can start marketing the home.

Do keep in mind you won't have to fix every little thing to sell a property you've purchased on short sales.

You will want to repair major issues, if they exist, and clean up cosmetic problems for faster resale, however. When dealing with contractors to get estimates, take the time to:

• **Explain your situation**

Some contractors will not give estimates if they can't "see" the work. If you explain your situation, they will be more likely to give a ballpark figure.

While this isn't as good as a full estimate, it will give you something to work with.

- **Vet contractors like you are ready to hire them**

If you do plan to go ahead with a deal, it's a good idea to start creating a real list of contractors in advance. This will help you with hiring when you're ready. To properly vet contractors, check into their licensing, their reputations and their level of experience.

- **Obtain at least three quotes per project**

Yes, this will take some work, but it can better help you with your estimations. Plus, it will speed up the process down the road when you're ready to hire contractors to get your purchase ready for resale. You'll be able to weed out those who come in way too high in advance and select others to consider.

If you really want to make money with a foreclosure short sale, you must do your homework in advance of a purchase. This means you'll still need an appraisal, an inspection and even construction estimates. Go into a purchase blind and you could end up seeing the profits you imagined going right down the drain along with thousands of dollars in plumbing repairs!

"A manager is not a person who can do the work better than his men; he is a person who can get his men to do the work better than he can".

-. Fred Smith (FedEx)

DEALING WITH FIXER UPPERS

Buying a short sale property isn't like purchasing a new home. There will very likely be a thing or two that will need to be done to any buy to make it sell faster. In some cases, the property will be best described as a fixer upper. This is okay, if you know how to handle it to keep as much money in your pocket at the end of the deal as possible.

Before diving into repairs with a fixer upper, you will want to assess the necessary repairs and cosmetic improvements that need to be made. If you are working on a budget, review them for what is absolutely necessary. Also consider what work you can do on your own and which projects will require a contractor.

If you've done your homework in advance of the purchase, the repair work should go rather smoothly. While you'll want to go through the quoting process – for real this time – you should have a good list of professionals to start with.

HIRING CONTRACTORS

For projects that you can't tackle on your own or simply do not want to handle, pull out that list of contractors you've already talked to and vetted. Now is the time to get real estimates and let them see the property to give their quotes in writing.

To hire the best contractor for the job, you'll want to:

- **Consider the quotes that come back**

To get the highest return down the road, you'll want to go with the lowest quote. As long as you have already vetted the contractors and know their work is solid, you should be perfectly okay in going with the lowest quote.

- **Find the contractor who can do the work the fastest**

When you're looking at short sale purchases to buy and then resell, time is money. The longer you hang onto the property, the more it will cost you.

- **Negotiate a contract**

Don't let major work start on your purchase until you have a contract in place. The contract should include details of the project, the agreed upon pricing, the materials involved and the estimated date of completion. If deadlines are important, which is always the case in investment property, make sure the contract includes penalties for failure to finish the work on time or at least provisions for enacting penalties.

Sometimes you have to hold contractors' feet to the fire to get a job done on time. Do bear in mind, however, that outside work on the structure could be delayed due to weather. This is, of course, beyond a contractor's ability to control.

Hiring contractors to get the work going should not be a very big issue for you as long as you did due diligence for yourself in the pre-purchase phase.

To expedite matters, work with the list you've already created and make sure the property is made available when contractors need it open. If you can't be there personally to let them in and supervise work, designate a representative to do so.

Doing Some Of The Work Yourself

If you are in the least bit capable of doing some of the work, you will find this is the best way to save yourself money. It will require some of your time, but it can add up to big savings in your final bottom line on a short sale purchase.

Some of the things you might be able to tackle include:

• **Handling the cosmetic issues**

If a house needs painting on the inside, chances are you can tackle the job. This could save you thousands of dollars in hiring painting crews. Other cosmetic issues that can be handled in-house, so to say, include minor drywall repairs, carpentry repairs and even just changing out switch plates and outlet covers for a cleaner, more uniform appearance.

• **Tackling the pre-showing cleaning**

Unless you have it in your budget to hire a cleaning crew once all repairs are made, chances are tackling this job personally will save you some time and a fair amount of cash.

• **Other issues**

Depending on your level of do-it-yourself expertise, you might be able to handle bigger repairs. Some investors have been known to lay their own carpeting, fix or replace roofs, retile bathrooms and even paint the outside of houses they buy. Just make sure whatever jobs you take on fall within your comfort zone. There's no point in biting off more than you can chew to save a bit of money. Do the job wrong and you'll waste your time and the cash for materials and you still mind end up having to hire a pro to get the job done!

DON'T FORGET THE CURB APPEAL

While your first priorities in getting a house ready for resale will, no doubt, lie in fixing any major problems and cosmetic issues within the home, don't forget the outside.

There is a lot to be said for curb appeal when it comes to reselling a piece of property.

The more tailored and inviting a home is on the outside, the more interested potential buyers are likely to be.

To boost the curb appeal, you will want to do a few things to the outside of a property:

- **Touch up or completely repaint the outside**

If a house is older, this is a very good idea. The cleaner and fresher the paint, the more appealing a house will be. If repainting isn't called for, consider pressure washing to put the outside into more pristine condition.

- **Take care of the lawn**

Keep the lawn outside of the home in good shape while you're in the resale process. If it needs replacing, do so. Otherwise, keep it edged, mowed, watered and green. Hire a service if this is a job you can't handle. Should you be dealing with snowy conditions, just keep the property clean and the snow shoveled for better showing.

- **Consider landscaping**

Adding a few trees, shrubs and flowers to the property can be very useful for boosting curb appeal if the season is right. You don't have to go overboard on this front, but a little bit can go a long way.

• **Don't overlook the backyard**

Making the front yard a showplace and leaving the back in a state of disarray can backfire on you. Making sure this is at least neat and tidy is a good idea. Don't worry about a lot of landscaping back here as many buyers will want wide open spaces to mold as they wish. Make sure it's manicured and pleasant to look at and you should be okay.

• **Repair the fence, if necesary**

Nothing can ruin the appearance of a property on the outside faster than a fence that's dirty, old or falling down. Wooden privacy fences that are in good repair can often be pressure washed for an instant face lift. Painting might also be called for. Replace only if it's 100 percent necessary. Chain link fencing that is rusted might need to be replaced.

If it's your intent to turn a short sale house back over as quickly as possible, getting it ready for resale will be imperative. Making at least some of the repairs and putting the house in good order visually can be extremely important. So can making the house look homey for potential buyers. Staging can help on this front.

"Have the courage to follow your heart and intuition. They somehow already know what you truly want to become. Everything else is secondary".

-. **Steve Jobs (Apple)**

STAGING FOR FASTER SALES

When the deal is closed, the repairs have been made and a purchase is almost as pretty as a picture, it's time to make it so. To entice potential buyers into making an offer and closing a deal, it can help to make your property more visually appealing on the inside. Since your short sale purchase won't show like a home that is occupied by an owner, you will want to make it look like it is – almost.

Studies have shown that vacant houses just don't appeal to buyers as much as homes that have objects in them. Furniture in the right places, a few pictures on the walls, drapes at the windows and a few other homey touches can make all the difference in the world. If you've ever wondered why builders put furnishings into model homes, this is the reason. The art is called staging and it can help you sell your home faster and even get higher offers in the process.

THE ART OF STAGING

Staging involves setting up a house to look like a "model home." Builders do this all the time to move their properties faster and more effectively. The trick with staging is to give the potential homebuyers just enough by way of furniture and accessories to be able to picture themselves living in the home, but not enough to make them envision someone else doing so.

Staging basically involves putting enough furniture and accessories into a home to make sure it doesn't have a Spartan look. The arrangements should be neutral, but eye pleasing. There's no need to crowd things.

The idea is to give buyers an idea of how a home would look if it was occupied by them. It can also help put them into an ownership frame of mind where they start envisioning how they could better arrange things to suit their needs. Psychologically, this is a very good thing to have happen while showing a home.

When it comes to staging, there are two major ways to get the job done. You can either hire a pro to set up a home to look more appealing, or you can try to do it yourself. Hiring a pro might cost you a little more, but it can pay off with more of a decorator's touch. Going it alone will take some creativity on your part, but it can save you money in the long run. If you intend on buying and selling short sales on a regular basis, learning the ropes and making investments in furniture and accessories to reuse can be wise.

HOW TO FIND A PRO

If you opt to hire a pro, you'll find that most major and many minor real estate markets have plenty of experts willing to help you.

To find a staging expert, consider checking with interior decorators, as this is right up their alley. If you've already contacted a real estate agent to help with the sale, there's a very good chance that agency can put you in touch with a staging expert. There's also a very good chance they've recommended that you take this step.

To find a good staging professional, you'll want to check into these things:

- **Their level of experience**

Overall, staging is a relatively new phenomena, but it's not new enough that so-called experts in the field won't have recommendations to their credit. Look at their experience level and check into their recommendations. You want to find a pro that has a track record of getting the job done right.

- **The services they offer**

A full-service staging professional will help you will all aspects of decorating and populating a home for resale. The best have contracts with rental places for furniture or even have their own warehouses packed with items to help them stage a home room by room.

• **Their pricing**

Staging can be expensive, but it shouldn't be outrageous in pricing. After all, you're not buying the furniture, the window dressings and the decorating touches. Rather, you're borrowing or renting them for a time.

Do put in the effort to interview a few different experts if they are available. Take a look at the designs they've put into place for other home sellers, too.

Ultimately, you want an expert that knows his or her stuff, but you don't want to be taken to the cleaners in the process.

DOING IT YOURSELF

Staging is, of course, a process you can tackle completely by yourself. As long as you have access to furniture and accessories or you can rent them, you should be on the right track. Remember, when it comes to staging, less is often more. You will want to make rooms look livable, but you won't want to go overboard with decorations and packing rooms full of furniture. Simple is best. As you try to stage the property yourself, don't forget these things:

• To furnish every room

Making sure every room shows well is ultimately a very good idea. You don't need to pack rooms full of things, but you do want to give buyers a good idea of how rooms will work with furnishings in them.

• Cover the windows

Even very simplistic window treatments will work better for you than having them left open, exposed and looking stark.

• The walls

You won't want to cover the walls from ceiling to floor with pictures and accessories, but a few touches in each room can go a very long way.

- **Other visual accessories**

Put a few things that make sense on counters, on top of furniture and so on. You will make the property look homey and inviting by doing this.

- **Avoid personal effects**

The idea behind staging is to make potential buyers feel at home. You don't want them to view the property as your home, however. Keep personal effects, photographs and other sentimental type things out of the process entirely. These things can shatter any illusion you are trying to create for a potential buyer.

- **Your budget**

Do keep your budget in mind as you stage. While you want to attract potential buyers, you don't want to kill your profit margin either. If you plan on buying more properties down the road, however, hang on to the decorations and accessories you buy for future use. This can help you get more bang for your buck eventually.

When buyers walk into a completely empty house, they see a shell. Many cannot see past this at the possibilities. Staging simply helps get buyers' imaginations working in the right direction. Even a few very simple touches can go a long way toward helping you sell a home and close a deal.

"It is impossible to win the race unless you venture to run, impossible to win the victory unless you dare to battle".

-. Rich DeVos (AMWAY)

GOING FOR THE EXIT

You have found your short sale property, checked it out nine ways to Sunday, closed the deal and readied the house for sale.

Good for you!

Now it's time to get your money and profit back out of the deal. Planning an exit strategy should begin even before you close the deal, but putting it into action should come when you're ready to start showing the property for real.

To make the most out of your exit and even speed up the process, you may want to consider doing such things as:

- **Setting the price with a modest profit margin**

Unless you are very positive you can get every penny of profit possible out of a house based on market conditions at the time you list, do be reasonable about setting the price. List the home with a profit amount that is higher than what you can live with, of course.

This will give you room for negotiations. If the house is worth $200,000 and your total investment with purchase, repairs and staging falls at $120,000, consider a fair amount somewhere in between. Ask for the full $200,000 and stick to it firm and you could find yourself waiting a very long time to earn that $80,000. Settle for $60,000 and you could be working on your second short sale purchase with money in the bank in no time at all.

- **Hiring an agent**

You can, of course, handle the resale on your own. This can slow down your sale timeframe, however. When a reputable agent is used to market the property effectively, you could see your money much faster.

- **Getting creative with advertising**

Do keep in mind that even in a fast-moving market there are generally a lot of properties for sale. You'll want to get creative with your marketing to generate leads and make a sale as fast and clean as possible.

- **Being open to negotiations**

This goes back to pricing, but it cannot be stressed enough. People often expect to negotiate on pricing. Don't set your listing exactly at the amount you need or want. This won't leave you wiggle room and it could wreck your chances to counteroffer with potential buyers.

- **Being patient**

Even in a bull market, you might have to exercise a little patience. Homes just don't sell over night very often. Make sure you have it in your plan to wait a while to make a sale. If the timing drags out too much, consider reducing your asking price by a small amount.

Try to avoid renting the property, if at all possible, if your ultimate goal is a resale. If your initial plan was to buy, hold and rent, then by all means pursuit it. Otherwise, you are likely to sell much faster if you don't muddy the waters with rental agreements and tenants getting in the way.

• **Being prepared**

While you will often get very fast nibbles on a property that has been purchased via short sale and listed with a low or reasonable price, there are no guarantees in the market. You do need to be prepared to pay the mortgage, taxes and other expenses for a time. Getting a great deal only to lose it because of bad financial planning in advance can be tragic.

"Great ambition is the passion of a great character. Those endowed with it may perform very good or very bad acts. All depends on the principles which direct them".

-. Napoleon Bonaparte (French General)

THE BOTTOM LINE ADVANTAGE

Purchasing property through short sales can be an excellent way to make serious money in the real estate market. You do need to be reasonable in your expectations, however. If you do your homework in advance of a purchase, make an offer that is reasonable and put in a little work after the sale, you will make money.

For many investors, short sales result in thousands of dollars in profits when all is said and done. Most see five-digit returns. Some, however, go for quantity over massive profits to make their money. The idea behind their philosophy is that a $5,000 or $8,000 profit for a few weeks of work beats spending that much time in an office. They're right! These same investors are also often the ones that buy one property, fix it up, sell it for a small profit and then turn right back around and do it again.

When it comes to real estate and previously occupied properties, the name of the game is coming out in the black. Pushing this number higher, of course, is always a big boost, but anticipating huge returns isn't always realistic if you want to sell fast.

Modest is more than acceptable in regard to returns. This is especially so if you intend to get right back in and work on another property to buy and sell.

To keep your expenses as low as possible and boost your bottom line margin as you're starting out in short sale purchases, make sure to:

- **Research your purchases carefully**

Not every great deal turns out to be so great in the end. Do take the time to make sure a value really adds up. Inspect properties, research neighborhoods and get a very good feel for the marketability of a particular purchase.

• **Do as much of the work as possible personally**

The more "experts" you can cut out deals, especially as you become more adept at buying and seller, the higher your profits are likely to be. Don't shy away from using experts when you need them, but do handle as much as you can to keep your initial costs lower.

• **Position yourself financially to wait for a time**

While short sale purchases often come cheap, you will still likely have to invest some time waiting for resale. Do not let yourself be caught blind here.

Short sales can give you a big bottom line advantage over other real estate purchases. Take your time, learn the ropes and you should see real profits adding up fast.

"Of the realization of each, depends the destiny of all".

-. Alexander Magno (King of Macedonia)

TO SELL OR NOT TO SELL

In today's market, flipping is not going to net you the payday that people were getting when the residential real estate market was booming towards the end of the last century. You can, however, end up selling the property and making a few thousand dollars for your efforts. You have the following choices when it comes to the property that you purchase on the short sale:

• Sell it as is and take any profit

• Fix it up and possibly sell it for more money than you can as is

• Rent it out

• Live in the property

The first two options are short term investments and the last two are long term investments. The residential real estate market today is better for the long term investment, however, you can still make money on a short term basis if you negotiated the short sale properly and got a good deal.

Sell it as is

If you sell it as is, you should try to do this by owner. Hold an open house and sell it for less than the market value. You may want to make some cosmetic changes to make it more appealing. You purchased the property for less than the market value so if you are not looking to make a killing, you can make a profit by 48 selling it under the market value.

Fix it up and sell it

If you are in the trades or know someone who is willing to work to fix up the property, this can be a better option. You can make all of the necessary repairs and make the house more appealing. Be sure to concentrate on cosmetic effects as this is what people notice more than those that are more expensive and add value to the home. If you have a choice between new carpeting and new windows, new carpeting will sell them every time, although new windows will actually add to the value of the home. New carpeting is a lot cheaper, too. Fixing it up and selling the property only works if you can do the bulk of the work yourself. If you are planning on contracting the work out, you may end up spending more than the house is worth.

Rent the house out

Before you do this, you should study the market, see the comparable rents and make sure that the rent you charge will cover the mortgage and taxes and leave a little left over for repairs. You are better off to enter into a "rent to own" agreement than just renting the property. This is because people tend to take better care of property that they are renting to own rather than just renting.

Renting out the house can be a good way to pay for the mortgage. Even if you paid cash for the property, you can finance it after closing, take the interest deduction off on your taxes (although you will have to claim the rent) and hold onto the property for a longer term. If you anticipate the property values rising (if the home is in a nice area, chances are very good the value of the home will accelerate once the housing industry gets back on its feet - which it always does), then this can be a smart long term investment.

Live in the home

If you are looking for a house in which to live, the short sale may be the best option you can get. You can get a house at less than market value and hold onto it for as long as you want. You can gradually fix it up over the years As we all need a place to live, this is a viable option for you. In this case, this can be a long term investment that really works out.

Real estate is a good investment. It is unlike stock, which is really just shares in a company. It is a tangible asset that is needed by everyone. We all need shelter so real estate is not about to go out of style. You just have to know how to invest, where to invest and when. Right now, investing in the short sale is the most lucrative form of real estate investing - regardless of whether you are looking long term or short term. Before you make your next 50 investment or buy a home, take a look at what you can get with a short sale real estate investment.

The Pros and Cons of Buying Foreclosure Short Sales

Are you interested in profiting from the growing number of mortgage borrowers who cannot pay their bills? If so, don't only examine foreclosures, but short sales too. Short sale properties are ones that will enter into foreclosure soon. Before that happens, mortgage lenders agree to sell the property for less than the outstanding mortgage due. They do this to move the process along, get a percentage of their money right away, and avoid costly and lengthy foreclosure proceedings.

Short sales are a great way to buy a cheap first home or turn a profit with flipping, but are they right for everyone? Not always. Like any other money making opportunity, the buying and reselling of short sale properties does have its pros and cons. So, what are they?

The Pros

You should get a good value for your money. Since short sales involve selling a property for less than the outstanding amount due on the mortgage, there is the potential to get a good value for your money. In dire circumstances, the home's appraised value is not considered, just the amount the lender will lose through foreclosure.

Can be less intimidating. If you want to buy an affordable property or a property to flip, your two cheapest options are foreclosures and short sales. Unfortunately, if you are new to the business, foreclosures can be intimidating. This is particularly true with foreclosure auctions. They are often jam packed full of professional investors and the auctions move at a fast pace. On the other hand, short sales involve dealing directly with a mortgage lender, real estate agent, or both.

You can turn a profit. The best chance of profiting from short sales is with flipping. You buy a property, make improvements, and resell for a profit. To make a profit, you need to spend a little as possible.

The Cons

You may not get the best price. As previously stated, short sales are a good value for the money. With that said, you may still pay a lot for a property. It is important to look at the big picture. Consider the home's appraised value. Say it is $450,000 and the borrowers still owe $300,000, and you are able to purchase the property for $275,000. $275,000 is a lot of money to pay for a home, but remember its $450,000 value. Although you pay a lot, it is a great value for the money.

Short sales do take time. Mortgage lenders have the final say in short sale approval. Unfortunately, some drag their feet. This is common when a property has two mortgages and by two different lenders. Both must agree to a short sale. The longest decision will be from the second mortgage company, as they are shorted. Some short sale buyers have waited as long as six months to receive a response. If you cannot or do not want to wait that long, apply pressure after a few weeks or month. State you are interested in the property, but losing interest. Request a decision in two weeks or else withdraw your purchase offer.

The short sale deal can fall apart. As with other real estate sales, the deal can fall apart. This is why most lenders take their time accepting an offer. They review the home's appraised value and estimate how much they can get from a lender owned home or a foreclosure auction.

Borrowers also have up to the final closing stages to make good on their outstanding mortgage. So, if a lender receives a better offer or if the borrower comes into the money, the deal can fall apart at the last minute.

Pros and Cons of Buying Short Sales as First Homes

In terms of short sales and foreclosures, a lot of focus is placed on profits. Yes, if you invest money into foreclosures and short sales, you should turn a profit.

There is however one aspect that many rarely take into consideration. That is buying a first home. If you are a hopeful homeowner who is operating on a limited budget or if you just want to limit your costs, foreclosures and short sales should be examined. Anymore can make a purchase offer. They aren't just for investors.

Now that you know it is possible for anyone to buy short sale properties, is it the right choice for you? It depends. Using short sales to buy a first home does have its pros and cons. What are they?

The Pros

A good value for the money. If you didn't already know, short sales are properties sold for less than the outstanding mortgage due. For mortgage lenders and borrowers, they are ideal alternatives.

Mortgage borrowers avoid embarrassment and the negative financial consequences of foreclosures. Mortgage lenders are able to avoid long and costly foreclosure proceedings. Since most homeowners owe less than the value of their home, you get a good deal.

For example, if the outstanding mortgage is for $120,000, you could expect to pay around $100,000. This does seem high, but not when you get a property valued at over $200,000. You still benefit from covering the outstanding mortgage.

Most homes are well-kept. Of course, you will need to make needed upgrades and repairs. Homeowners who are unable to pay their mortgage, are unlikely to afford repairs and upgrades. The home may need a new roof, new carpeting, and so forth. With that said, most homes are in good condition.

Homeowners with delinquent mortgages care about their homes, they just can't afford them any longer. With foreclosures, you get squatters. These delinquent buyers refuse to leave the home without force. These disgruntled persons are likely to damage property, as they honestly don't care anymore.

Can later be resold for a profit. If you are looking to buy a cheap first home, your goal is to get a good deal now. Don't discount the future financial benefits of short sale properties. Since you get a good value for your money, you automatically profit.

Using the above mentioned example, if you purchase a home with an appraised $200,000 value for only $100,000 you automatically profit from the resale.

Add in years of improvements and upgrades and that value should only increase.

The Cons

The process does take time. Most mortgage lenders consider short sales a last ditch effort to avoid foreclosure. They take time to accept a purchase offer. During that time, they are comparing short sales with foreclosure and possibly waiting for a better offer. Some report waiting more than six months for lender approval. Luckily, if you are renting you are in a relatively good position. Negotiate with your current landlord. Let them know you are in the process of trying to buy a property. If you have history of being a good and paying tenant, they may operate on a month-by-month basis.

The cost is higher than foreclosures. Typically, foreclosures have lower selling prices. As previously stated, short sales give you a good value for your money. This is because you get a relatively well-kept for home without going through an intimidating and fast paced foreclosure auction.

So, should you buy a short sale property as a first home? The decision is yours to make. It won't hurt to look, but if you goal is to avoid intimidating foreclosure auctions and get the best value for your money, foreclosure short sales should be closely examined.

"Purity of heart is what enables us to see".

-. Jesus de Nazareth (Profets)

CONCLUSIONS ABOUT SHORT SALE

The stories you have heard about short sales are true. Banks will sell properties for less than what is owed in a loan. To make the most of these deals, you need to strike while the iron is hot. Act quickly and without cutting corners and you could find yourself sitting on mini-goldmines of potential. Drag your feet and another investor might step in or a bank might choose to go ahead with foreclosure.

Making money on foreclosure short sales does take some work. If you think the process will be completely easy, you're fooling yourself. If you take your time, put in the research and effort, however, the profits can make the elbow grease seem very worthwhile.

Buying and selling real estate is never an exact science. To get the most out of this prospect, it is often best, at least initially, to surround yourself with professionals who can lend you their expertise along the way. If you need help finding a property to buy or marketing it, hire a Realtor. If you have legal questions, take the plunge and hire a lawyer. Should a property need repairs you can't handle, get a contractor. The more thorough you are on the front end, the more likely it is you will be able to sell with reasonable expediency and get a nice profit in the process.

5 Reasons to Examine Short Sales

Are you looking to become a first-time homeowner? If so, you may turn to foreclosures to save money. Unfortunately, foreclosure auctions are often jam packed full of professional investors. Yes, you can still try to buy a home in foreclosure, but the best option is to opt for a foreclosure short sale instead.

A foreclosure short sale is when the borrower and the lender agree to quickly sell the home. It is used as an alternative to foreclosure. To avoid poor credit markings and to avoid lengthy and costly foreclosure proceedings, both parties usually agree to a short sale. To quickly sell the home, its price is greatly reduced.

Some mortgage lenders do take the home's appraised value into consideration, but others opt for an amount near or smaller than the outstanding amount due on the mortgage.

So, why should you, as a hopeful first-time homeowner, target foreclosure short sales?

1 – Wide Range of Properties Available for Sale

It is most common to see single-family homes offered for sale via a short sale. With that said, you never know. Landlords are also struggling with the poor economy. Some are making poor financial choices and others are stuck with non-paying tenants.

Not only can you find single-family homes for sale via short sales, but multi-family homes too. If you not only want to own a home, but profit too, live in one of the apartment and rent the other.

2 – Cheap Properties

As previously stated, foreclosure short sales are an alternative to foreclosures. Mortgage lenders have accepted the fact the borrowers cannot and will not pay them. Instead of taking a total lost and spending months and thousands of dollars in foreclosure proceedings, they agree to a short sale. In doing so, they are willing to take a small loss.

This results in cheap properties for you.

Yes, short sale properties are sold at a reduced rate, but be cautious of those sold through deceitful lenders or real estate agents. They try to up the price and make more money.

Before agreeing to a foreclosure short sale, compare the selling price with the home's appraised value. It should be less.

3 – Typically Well-Kept Homes

Borrowers who approach their lender for a short sale are responsible individuals. They have just fallen on hard times. They are concerned with the short-term and long-term financial impacts of foreclosure.

These individuals care, unlike those who sit in a home that they cannot afford waiting for an eviction notice.

What does this mean for you? It typically means a well-kept home.

Those who opt for foreclosure short sales care about themselves, their reputation, and take pride in their home. They just can't afford it any longer.

These individuals take care of the property.

On the other hand, it is not uncommon for those who receive an eviction notice during foreclosure to become unruly and even damage the property.

In this instance, it means costly repairs.

4 – Can Profit Later

If you are a hopeful first-time homeowner, your goal is to find an affordable home, not make a profit. With that said, don't forget about the long-term aspect. In five or ten years, you may wish to purchase a new home or relocate across the country.

This involves a home sale. If you only paid $100,000 for a home valued at $200,000, you automatically make a profit. Throughout the years of owning and living in the home, upgrades are likely. These upgrades will only increase the home's value, meaning more profit for you.

5 – Bargaining Power

If you are in good financial standing, have the ability to obtain financing, or have the needed financial resourced on hand, you are in a good position to bargain. If you know the property is being sold as a short sale, research the home's appraised value.

This should be on file with the mortgage lender, real estate agent, and should be public record. If you aren't getting what you deem to be a good deal, bargain. If dealing directly with the mortgage lender, ask about obtaining financing through them. This result in a continuing relationship. If you have the needed financial resources on hand, state your price and offer to make payment right then and there.

Finally;

Thank you for taking the time to read this book and I want to be at your service to help you in any step or position in front of a foreclosure, either to avoid it or to acquire a property through a short sale.